# About the a

Rita Haworth lives and works in the north of England. She is a retired senior university lecturer who was born with a special gift. Rita is the author of a number of academic publications, but this is the first time she has penned her lifelong journey as a psychic medium. Taking early retirement to focus more on her service to the spirit world, Rita now spends her days doing psychic readings and helping people communicate with their loved ones who have gone before them. Rita's main aim is to bring comfort, compassion and peace of mind to all those who seek out her service.

# AMBASSADOR FOR SPIRIT

# RITA HAWORTH

---

## AMBASSADOR FOR SPIRIT

Vanguard Press

VANGUARD PAPERBACK

© Copyright 2022
**Rita Haworth**

The right of Rita Haworth to be identified as author of
this work has been asserted by her in accordance with the
Copyright, Designs and Patents Act 1988.

A CIP catalogue record for this title is
available from the British Library.

ISBN 978 1 80016 348 5

*Vanguard Press is an imprint of
Pegasus Elliot MacKenzie Publishers Ltd.*
www.pegasuspublishers.com

First Published in 2022

**Vanguard Press
Sheraton House Castle Park
Cambridge England**

Printed & Bound in Great Britain

# Dedication

I would like to dedicate this book to the spirit world and all those who inspired me to put pen to paper.

# Acknowledgements

I would sincerely like to thank the spirit world for choosing me to serve them. I would also like to thank Gary, Nicola, Barbara, Arthur, John, David, Eileen, Glyn and Robert, my wonderful family for all your love. I would also like to thank my many friends and colleagues from over the years who have helped me get this far. Special thanks go to Jim Byrne and Julie Atkins for all your guidance and teaching along my spiritual journey and last, but not least, my friend and long-time colleague Karen Kinghorn for being the earth angel that you are.

# Contents

# Introduction

This is the true story of one girl's journey to overcome adversity. Born into a family of eight, she had to grow up fast following a traumatic event in her childhood. By the age of nineteen she was married, a mother and stuck in a dead-end job. It was a 'chance' meeting with a medium and the unexpected death of a family member that led to a major reassessment of her life. She set off on a journey that would not only change her life for the better but thousands of others too. She went from a girl who left school with almost no qualifications to a woman with a professional career and a very special gift. Despite heartbreak and setbacks, she began to train as a spirit medium in her twenties. In her thirties, she went on to gain two degrees; a first-class honours degree in community studies and a postgraduate master's degree in social policy, both welfare related. She knows that everything that has happened in her life has been guided by spirit. Some events have come as blessings, some have come as lessons, everything she knows has a reason. Throughout the following pages you will be gripped by Rita's story. A chance meeting with her dead friend in the middle of the night set her on an unusual path. Her deceased friend told her she had an interesting life ahead of her where she would help thousands of people. At the time Rita dismissed this idea; she could hardly help herself back then let alone help others. It was that 'chance' meeting with Jim Byrne, a Spiritual medium, one night many years later that would change her life forever.

In the following pages, Rita hopes to spread some inspiration and show that physical death, though painful and sometimes heart-breaking for those left behind, is never really the end. She has made it her life's work to be a bridge between the two worlds, delivering messages of hope and reassurance. Those who have left us might have died physically but spirit always lives on.

# Chapter 1
## The journey begins

I arrived in the world one dreary day in March 1959, daughter of Barbara and Arthur. The second of six children, the early years were mostly happy. As each of the following four children arrived, the small resources we had needed to stretch further. We didn't have a lot, but we had each other. When I was five, I got stuck in a sewerage pipe whilst playing hide and seek and needed to be rescued by the fire service. This incident coincided with my first ever feelings of fear. I was mostly a carefree soul and my eldest brother John, and I spent hours playing on 'cardboard hill'. We cadged old cardboard boxes from the neighbours, ripped them into squares and used them as magic carpets to slide down the hill over and over again. Sometimes in the school holidays we would take jam sandwiches with us and stay out for hours on end playing on a rope swing or paddling in the river. Back then people didn't worry about their kids whereabouts like they do today.

One night when I was nine, I went to bed just like any other night without a care in the world. Mum and Dad had gone to visit my nan and 'Aunty Glady', not my real aunt but someone in my childhood who I loved dearly, was babysitting. Rather than drifting off into a deep slumber as I usually did, I felt restless and as I lay there in the dark, I began to feel butterflies in my stomach, and I could see small flashing white lights all around the room. I got an overwhelming feeling that something wasn't right. I had never experienced anything like it. As I became mesmerised by the light I feel into a deep sleep. Sometime later I was woken by a huge bang. I jumped from the bed as fast as a cheetah and threw back the curtains. My little eyes could not believe what they were seeing. Surely, I must still be asleep, and this must be a terrible dream? There she was, my mother lying on the road, my dad's car about seventy yards further back, mangled round a concrete lamppost. My little brain couldn't compute what was happening, so I slid back into bed and went fast to sleep. I wasn't asleep long before I felt my aunt gently shaking me awake, I will never forget the horrified look on her tear-stained face. I could see the reflection of the emergency service lights in the window. The real nightmare had just begun. They cut Dad out of the car and scooped Mum off the road. I later learned Dad had swerved to miss a car that came out of a side street, skidded and landed up hitting the lamppost head on.

Dad seemed to be in hospital for months and I wasn't allowed to see him. Mum was home within a few weeks but was in a bed that had been set up for her in the lounge. The first time I saw her I was horrified, the fear I had felt when stuck in the pipe at age five had returned. Mum was swaddled in bandages from head to toe and looked like an Egyptian mummy. This was to cover the horrific cuts sustained when she went through the windscreen. Grandma and Grandad, or Nan and Pop as I liked to call them, were called in to look after us kids. Routine returned to normal. Well, as normal as it could be in the circumstances. I returned to school but, instead of skipping there, I found myself shuffling along, looking at the floor and missing my dad.

My tenth birthday came and went and the best present I could have wished for was when Nan told me Dad was coming home. I stood on the front doorstep moving from one leg to the other in anticipation, waiting for him to arrive; the excitement was overwhelming. The man who had gone out that fateful night to visit my nan was not the same man who arrived home. The happy loving person I used to hide behind when I was shy had gone and in his place was a depressed shadow of himself. Life as we all knew it would never be the same. By the age of twelve, I could cook, clean and look after my siblings. Mum and Dad would often fight, and I had to grow up fast.

By the time I was sixteen, I had gone off the rails a bit, I wasn't performing very well at school and spent more time chasing boyfriends than doing homework. I left school with hardly any qualifications but, somehow, managed to secure a place at the local catering college. It was whilst doing this course that my classmates and I went to a catering fair in London. Arriving home later that evening I was greeted by my mum wafting the local paper under my nose. I looked down at the page to see a picture of my best friend looking back at me. As I read the headline, I couldn't believe what I was reading, 'Young man loses his life as his girlfriend fights for life'. As the tears rolled down my face that feeling of dread was welling up in my stomach again. Janine died four days later aged just sixteen; the grief I felt was beyond devastating.

As I lay in bed a few nights later, thinking about the motorbike accident that had taken one of the funniest girls I had ever known, I began to see flashing lights around the bedroom just like I had on the night of my parents' crash. I began to get particularly drawn to one of the lights hovering just below the ceiling. As I became transfixed, I could see the outline of a person materialising. As clear as day, I saw Janine standing there fooling around just as she always had. Without any words, kind of mind to mind, she said she was fine now and not to worry as good things were being planned for my future and I was destined to help thousands of people. At the time I was a bit dubious about what I had seen and what Janine had said. I could hardly help myself at the time never mind helping others.

By the time I was eighteen I was married to a local lad. At nineteen I became a mother and by the time I was twenty-five I was divorced and living back home with my dad. Mum, by now, had left after years of Dad's depression and had gone in search of some happiness whilst she still could.

Whilst living back home, my brother Glyn introduced me to a friend of his called Jim. I didn't know it then, but Jim was going to have a profound effect on my life. Jim, I learned, was a spiritualist medium and I was fascinated to learn more. I had been reading playing cards and tarot cards for friends since I was a teenager. I never had any training to do this, I just looked at the cards and said what came into my mind. People would report back and tell me what I had said when reading for them had come true. For me, at this time, it was just a bit of light-hearted fun and if people said my predictions came true, it was a bit of a bonus. Talking to Jim one evening he said he would be taking the divine service at the local spiritualist church the following Saturday and I should come along to see what he did. I had never been to a spiritualist church before, I don't think I had even heard there was such a thing. I had been brought up as Church of England and visited my local C of E church regularly when I was young, collecting lots of 'prizes' for good attendance. I had thought I might like to become a nun when I was older, but it wasn't meant to be.

The big night came and Jim and his mum, Betty gave me a lift to the local spiritualist church. Betty and I sat in the congregation and Jim disappeared into a side room. When he reappeared, he walked onto the platform at the head of the church. He said a prayer and we sang a hymn, similar to the proceedings of any other church I had attended, so no difference there. Then all of a sudden, he called out to a lady in the congregation and said, "Can I come to you please?" He started to describe the features of a gentleman and said he had passed to the spirit world after being ill for some time with a chest infection.

He asked the lady if she recognised the gentlemen he was describing and she said, "Yes, it's my husband!"

I was blown away. I always thought it was just me who could see dead people and I had never really told anyone about this in case they thought I was gaga. Jim went on to give messages from the spirit world to other people in the audience and before I knew it the service was over. As I looked up at the stained-glass window at the back of the platform, I saw a bright white light hovering in the corner. I just knew I would be back here soon.

Life trundled on. I would take my daughter to school, go and do my waitressing job and be back in time to pick her up. When I was twenty-six, we moved into our own little rented house. Consequentially or not, as the case would be, I lived quite close to the spiritual church where I had gone to watch Jim. One night, when Nic had gone to see her dad, I decided to take a visit to the church on my own. As I walked through the door, an overwhelming feeling descended on me. A feeling of peace and love surrounded me, and I felt like I had come home. On my way out after the service I looked up at a noticeboard and saw an advertisement which read 'spiritual development here every Wednesday at 7 p.m'. I wasn't sure what this entailed but I had a strong feeling I needed to be there.

Wednesday night arrived and I found myself occupying one of the seats that had been put out in the shape of a circle. A lovely lady I was later to learn was called Marlene stood up, said a short prayer and then asked us all to close our eyes. She talked us through a guided meditation that was very relaxing. As I opened my eyes, I couldn't believe what I was seeing. Not only the lights I had previously seen were there, but I could see the glow of colours swirling around the people sitting opposite me. I later learned this light around the body is called an aura and the white lights I had seen many times over the years were orbs, the build-up of spirit energy. People started to stand up and give messages from the spirit world to each other. Some people could take what was being said, others could not. My behind stayed on the chair that night and I didn't say a word, I was just feeling high from the phenomenon I witnessed. Walking home after church, the air was cool, and the full moon was bright, the calm I felt around me was overwhelming and I just knew I had found the right path.

I attended the Wednesday circle for the next three years and the divine service every Sunday. As I got more confident, I would stand up when it was my turn and give out messages. I just described what I saw in my mind, described a spirit and would relay what they had come to say. To say I was gobsmacked when people said they recognised the deceased person I was describing and that they understood the message I was conveying to them was an understatement. Throughout this time, I was invited by the church to participate in what they called a fledgling service. This was an opportunity to participate in taking a service under supervision in order to practice mediumship in front of an audience. The first time I stood up there my mouth was dry, and my stomach was in a knot. I was petrified I wouldn't receive any spirit communication and would just look foolish. I needn't have worried. As soon as I stood up to take my turn, the spirits were queuing up to come through. Before I knew it, my slot was over, and I learned that day to never doubt spirit again.

By 1986, things were still swinging along, my daughter was getting bigger, and, alongside my spiritual work, I was now working in a Greek restaurant. Life was good but sometimes I felt a little lonely. I hadn't had much of a relationship with anyone since my marriage had broken down. My friend Carol, who I worked with, decided we would have a night out; I had not had many nights out since I moved into my own house. As I sat with the other girls at work having lunch, I mentioned our up-and-coming trip to our local pub. Jokingly I said, "Pray I meet the man of my dreams tonight, ladies." We all giggled and got on with finishing our lunch. Little did I know what the spirit had in store for me. At the agreed time Carol and I met up and off to the local pub we went. I can still recall what I was wearing, cream sweater, black skirt and pink tights. Yes, I know, I really did have bright pink legs.

We got a drink and took our seats; I scanned the room to get my bearing and noticed to my right a group of guys playing dominos. One of the guys seemed to stand out; he was younger than the others and was wearing a white T-shirt and a ripped denim jacket. Every time I looked over, he was looking at me and then I was looking at him. We ended up smiling across the room at each other and eventually he offered to buy me a drink.

Carol made herself scarce and I landed up talking with him eye to eye all night. We began to see each other and eventually he moved in with me. My soulmate had arrived, and we are still together now thirty-five years later. I swear to this day that spirit brought us together. He was the yin to my yang, and I was, and still am, the softness to his strength. His name is Gary and he's the love of my life.

# Chapter 2
## And then the bomb dropped

We both worked hard and took what overtime we could get; within eighteen months we had saved enough for the deposit on our first new home together. By now it was 1989, my daughter liked Gary and we all got along like a proper little family. My bouts of loneliness had banished, and my confidence had begun to grow. I was still attending the spiritualist church and doing readings for those who came to me for reassurance.

Later that year I fell pregnant; we were both ecstatic and looking forward to the birth the following August. Alas, it wasn't meant to be. I started to bleed, the GP was called and as I was going for a scan the day after he told me to speak to the doctor at the hospital about it. The following day as I lay on the bed the stenographer ran the scanner over my stomach. I could see a concerned look on her face as she turned the screen with my baby's image on it away from me. I just knew in that moment my baby was dead. I saw a doctor who confirmed this. I was given an operation to remove the foetus and I went home feeling empty and heartbroken. My sister Eileen and Gary rallied round and looked after me. It hadn't been the way I wanted to celebrate my thirtieth birthday, but we don't always get what we want.

Life moved on and we got back into our usual routine. It was early June when I was standing at the bus stop waiting to make my way to work when a funeral procession passed. The same thing happened for the next two days. By the third time, I knew someone in the spirit world was trying to send me a message. That night I meditated and as my spirit guide came close to me, I felt an overwhelming sadness, the message being that someone I loved dearly was now in the spirit world. I still wasn't sure who it was as I hadn't had any news of a passing.

Two days later, Friday 9 June 1989, we were sitting in the lounge watching TV when someone knocked at the door. My mother and her partner stood there. I could tell from my mum's face it was bad news and as I looked past her shoulder, I could see the spirit outline of my brother Glyn standing at the back of her. She didn't need to tell me; I already knew Glyn was dead. He was just twenty-five years old. Glyn was always the bright one in the family; he was the only one of the six of us who went to grammar school, and he was also very gifted musically. By the time he was twenty-two he was already part of a duo; they called themselves Berlitz and would go on to make two records and be the warm-up group for Chaka Khan, a well-known popstar on her world tour.

When he returned from the tour, Glyn didn't seem himself. I couldn't put my finger on it, but I wondered if he had taken drugs whilst travelling with the jet set? This we will never know but his mental health began to decline. Eventually he was diagnosed with schizophrenia and sent home from hospital with anti-psychotic medication. He lived in his own little flat and my mother was concerned about this, however, his psychiatrist told her he would be fine now he had the right tablets and not to worry. How wrong he was. Glyn took extra medication to help him feel better; he landed up falling and banging his head. He never got up again, well, at least not in this world. His death was reported to the coroner and at the inquest an open verdict was recorded. As a consequence, we will never know exactly what really happened that fateful day. My Nan and Pop also passed over the same year, a few months apart. At least I had the comfort of knowing they were now looking after Glyn in the spirit world.

By this time, I had left the Greek restaurant I had worked at for ten years and was now working in the local library café. At break time I would go upstairs and browse the books. I had always loved books but never really had a lot of time to read them. One day, I was pouring out cups of tea when I looked up to see someone I used to waitress with years ago, standing in the queue. We began to chat, and I asked her what she was doing these days. She said she was studying for a master's degree. I was very impressed and said she must be really clever to be able to do that. She came right back at me and said, "It has nothing to do with being clever, it's about having the discipline and dedication to study." I thought whatever it is I'd never be able to do it given my poor performance at school. My next thought was interrupted by my manager telling me the fridge and the microwave needed cleaning. Over the next few weeks, I thought a lot about Shirley and all her achievements. How wonderful must it be to achieve such goals?

I was still visiting the spiritualist church and my mediumship was getting stronger. The deaths of Glyn, my grandparents and the loss of the baby led to me questioning my own life and what I was doing with it.

Whilst meditating I would ask my spirit guides and friends in the spirit world to show me the best way forward. There was no immediate response, but I was reminded of what Janine had said to me the night she visited me from the spirit world all those years ago. I thought if I am going to help people like she said, I had better get on with it. I was thirty years old by now and I had spent most of my working life waiting on tables and serving tea and sandwiches. I dreamed about becoming a full-time medium. However, working for myself wouldn't give me the regular income I was used to. I thought if spirit wants me to do this, they will help make the conditions right to enable me. Alas, for the time being they had a different plan. Life went on and I continued in my catering job and doing free readings for friends and friends of friends in the evenings.

One day, in July 1990, my manager called me into the office. She told me the café was to shut and we were all going to be made redundant. I would like to say I was upset and worried about where my next job was coming from but, for some strange reason, I was not. I phoned my old boss from the Greek restaurant I used to work at and asked if there were any vacancies. She was happy to hear from me and said I would be welcome back any time.

A couple of weeks later a flyer came through the letter box at home. The flyer was all about evening classes that would be available from September that year at the local college. Two courses in particular caught my eye: access to higher education and access to health and social care. I had grand ideas about becoming a social worker. I thought about the conversation I had had with Shirley a couple of years before, when she had said, "You don't need to be clever, you just need to be dedicated to your studies to succeed." That evening I talked it over with Gary and he encouraged me to give it a go. What was there to lose? If I failed, at least I will have given it a go. By September 1990, I was back waiting on tables at the Greek restaurant through the day and attending college and doing homework in the evening. I was a bit disappointed I still wasn't working as a full-time medium but at least I had college to look forward to.

The first time I walked into class I was introduced to my peers. The teacher went round the class asking us to introduce ourselves and explain what we currently did for a living. There was an accountant, a police officer, someone who worked in a children's home and a student nurse amongst others. I wondered what they would think when I said I was a waitress who hadn't studied since I was sixteen. I thought what am I doing here and wanted to bolt for the door. At break time I got chatting with some of the other students and saw how wrong I was. They all made me feel really welcome and there were friendships made that day that have lasted a lifetime.

After about three weeks I received my first assignment. We had to choose a question from the list provided and write a thousand-word essay on the given topic. I agonised over which question I would tackle and eventually chose one about euthanasia. The question was 'Should euthanasia be legalised'? We were advised to treat writing the essay like a court case, offering arguments for and against legalising euthanasia before coming to a conclusion. The piece needed to be referenced to show where the information being used came from. Given I hadn't studied since I was sixteen, I was tearing my hair out trying to get the words down on paper but, somehow, I managed to write the expected one thousand words. At the bottom of my work, I put a note on for the lecturer apologising for the poor standard of my work.

A week or so later it was feedback day. I dreaded opening the envelope. I thought they would say I'm not up to it and throw me off the course. However, I was pleasantly surprised I got a level three-mark, level four was the highest mark you could get and I was just one level below. My lecturer Jon Bishop had replied to the apologetic comment I had put at the bottom of the assignment. He said the essay was far from poor and he had marked ten times worse. With a bit of practice, he said I would soon be getting level four. That man boosted my confidence ten times more than any teacher had ever done before and it was his encouragement that pushed me on to the next level.

By November, Jon said it was time to fill in our applications for entry to university. I said I would pass on that one, as I was still not convinced I would pass this course let alone be able to study at university level. He encouraged me to fill in the form regardless, suggesting even if I didn't put it in now it would be good practice for me if I changed my mind later.

We were then advised what we needed to do in order to get ahead with our future career choices. I had my eye on becoming a social worker and was told I would need to do some voluntary work in a social care capacity in order to get on a social work course. Before I knew it, I was working as a voluntary associate at the local probation office. I helped to run a drop-in centre for offenders and wrote a regular newsletter called 'In Touch', aimed at keeping local people serving prison sentences in touch with what was happening back home in their local community. At last, I was doing something useful and helping people just as Janine had told me I would all those years ago when her spirit visited me in the bedroom that night.

By July 1991, I was really enjoying my voluntary work alongside still doing my day job. Around the same time, I received my final grades from the access course. It's hard to believe but I got top marks and now had a qualification which was equal to gaining two A levels. I was ecstatic and really had the study bug. I thought about what Jon had said about applying to university. I found a copy of the application I had filled in several months before in class and popped it in the post addressed to the local university admissions tutor.

I carried on working in probation in my spare time and was offered the post of part-time probation officer assistant. In my new role I was able to do more work with the service users. From doing this work I got a unique view of human nature. Many of the people I worked with were not bad, they had just made wrong choices. I continued to work in the probation service for a further three years. I then left unscathed; the only bad incident I had was when one of the clients, high on drugs, threatened to wrap a snooker cue around my head. This aside, I found my time in probation very rewarding and informative.

I would have liked to have stayed longer but, alas by now, life had taken yet another turn and I couldn't do everything. In August that year I received a letter from the university; I had been offered a place on a degree course to study community studies. The course was to start in just six weeks' time! At first, I thought how fantastic, then reality set in as I thought about the practicalities. Could we afford it? Who would look after Nicola? I went off to meditate and clear my head.

As I relaxed, I could feel spirit coming close. I always knew when they were there as they left what I call their calling card. I would get a tingling feeling around my chin. As I opened my eyes, I could see the outline of a hand on the ceiling. The hand was playing a keyboard and I knew straight away who the hand belonged to. It was my dearly departed brother Glyn. I was overwhelmed with emotion; I had tried to contact him since he passed in 1989 to no avail. Neither had I had a message from him through any of the mediums I had consulted. Although he didn't materialise fully on that occasion, I knew one hundred percent it was him. I asked him what I should do? He said I should not worry and go and do my degree as I would need it to help others in the future. I immediately thought he must be talking about me doing social work in the future. As his hand started to fade, I thanked him for being there for me. I now knew where I was going next, and I promised him I would do it for both of us.

# Chapter 3
## Putting the practice into place

I was still doing readings alongside my part-time waitressing job when I started my degree. We had talked through our finances and Gary said he would look after Nicola if I had to study in the evenings and my mum offered to help out with finances if we got stuck. I changed my work patten so I could work at weekends, freeing up time throughout the week so I could attend lectures and study. Some days I had to pinch myself. Was I now really a full-time university student? Who would have thought it?

I took to studying at this level like a duck to water. Although the course was demanding, I was determined to work hard and give it my best shot. After all, I wasn't just doing it for me, I was doing it for Glyn too, as promised. He had been robbed of the opportunity to succeed so doing it for both of us made me even more determined. I remembered what Jon, my old college lecturer, had taught me; to write assignments like it was a court case presenting both sides of the argument. This formula seemed to work for me and soon I was getting good grades. I had to put the hours in, but it seemed to be paying off. I made lots of new friends whilst studying but two stick out in my mind more than most. Cath and Ruth were great ladies, and they too were mature students like me. I would speak to Cath on the phone most days and we would discuss up-and-coming assignments and how we were going to tackle them. We would meet up with Ruth for breakfast on the days we were in uni. We all got on really well and it was nice to have support from people who knew what I was talking about. The first year of study flew by. I had to give up quite a bit of my social life, missing nights out and friends' parties in order to study but it was worth the sacrifice.

In the summer holidays I worked extra hours and we also went on holiday. We took a trip to Cyprus and the weather was scorching. We bought tickets to take a three-day mini cruise to Israel and Egypt. Israel was amazing, we went to Bethlehem and saw the place Jesus was said to have been born. We also visited the Wailing Wall in Jerusalem, a sacred place for Jews. People were writing prayers on scraps of paper and sticking them in the gaps between the bricks. I too also took the opportunity to do this, and I asked God to keep all my family safe and to help me succeed in my studies. As I looked at a model of the Star of David surrounded by lit candles, I could feel the pain and horror of the genocide that had taken place in Germany back in the 1940s.

Egypt was also really interesting too. We visited the pyramids in Giza, and I was lucky enough to go inside one. The energy I felt in there was electrifying and I could see the spirit of people buzzing about down there. Cairo museum was equally fascinating and full of Egyptian artefacts including the gold death mask of Tutankhamen.

Before I knew it, it was September again and time to start year two of my degree. I'd agreed to meet Cath and Ruth for breakfast in the refectory the day we started back. Cath arrived first and was looking refreshed after her summer break. Ruth arrived but I noted she looked tired. We had a quick chat about what we had all being doing over the break and then went off to a lecture.

A few weeks later I was seeing less and less of Ruth; she didn't turn up much for our breakfast get-togethers and was absent quite a lot from lectures. She was very bright and doing really well so I couldn't understand her absences. One day around mid-term when I did see her, I noticed she had lost weight. She was always big and bouncy, and I was a little taken aback to see her like this. I asked if she had been dieting. She said she had no need to diet as the weight was coming off due to cancer. My heart slumped for her. She had survived kidney cancer in her twenties; this time it had come back with a vengeance in her stomach. She took time off from the course and underwent chemotherapy for the next three months. Nine months later she was told her illness was terminal.

Cath and I were heartbroken for her; she had so much to live for. We made it our business to pick Ruth up each Friday when she felt up to it to go out for lunch. When she wasn't well enough to go out any more, we would visit her at home, taking lunch with us. In January 1992, she began to seriously deteriorate and was moved to a hospice. Cath and I continued to visit her there. The nurses were superb with her and would make afternoon tea for us all when we visited. The last time I saw her she put her arms out to me. I could feel her fear. I gave her a big hug and told her she would be fine, and I knew her grandma was waiting to welcome her home to the spirit world. Ruth passed two days later, aged thirty-eight, leaving behind three young children and a husband. I didn't see or hear from her for a long time after she passed but I did receive a message from her through a well-known medium, Gordon Smith one night at a demonstration he was doing. Cath and I missed Ruth so much but we both knew she would want us to crack on with our studies and that's what we did. I made a vow; I wasn't just doing my studies for me and Glyn, I was now doing it for Ruth too.

Alongside work and study, I was still attending the development circle at church and, occasionally, I would take the divine service on Sunday. We all have a spirit guide, sometimes referred to as a guardian angel. I met my spirit guide face to face around this time whilst meditating. Savanna appeared in my mind's eye as a nun. How strange, I thought, my friend and I used to dress up as nuns and play at church and prayers when we were little, As I said earlier, I thought I would have liked to be a nun when I grew up, but it wasn't to be. I asked Savanna about her life when she had walked on the earth plane. She had lived in eighteenth-century Italy, was brought up in Milan and served as a nun for almost forty years in Verona. Her mission in life was to serve God and help the sick and poor. I know it is hard to comprehend that I actually met my guide, but you need to bear in mind I had been developing to be a medium for over ten years now.

Savanna became my gatekeeper and would help me to bring messages of communication from those in the spirit world to those here who needed to hear them. People just tended to find me; many came to me through word of mouth. People would ring me day or night desperate to hear a message from their departed loved ones or wanted guidance on everyday problems.

I did lots of readings, but certain ones have stuck in my mind. For example, a young lady we will call Joan to protect her identity came for a reading. Joan had been trying to get into the police service. She had tried twice already but unfortunately wasn't accepted because she had failed the required physical test on both occasions. She had been told to work on her fitness and apply again for the final time in a few months. She had her heart set on becoming a police officer and needed to know if she would finally be accepted on her third attempt. I shuffled the cards and asked her to pick nine. As I laid the cards out to read them, it all looked positive till I turned the last two. I could feel Savanna drawing close and she had an elderly spirit lady with her with an Irish accent. I described the lady to Joan, and she said it sounded like her grandma. I already knew this but was looking for total confirmation. Most of the cards were favourable and showed she would get her wish. The final two cards that pointed to the future showed illness and death. Of course, I didn't tell her this and wished her well for her up-and-coming career in the police. As I was drawing to a close, I could see a man appearing in my mind's eye and could smell cigarette smoke quite strongly. I asked if he had a message for Joan. He said he was her dad, and he would be waiting to greet her when it was her time to come over. He also confirmed what the cards had said that she would get into the police. As he was fading, he said it would last for ten years. I told Joan her dad was around, helping her to reach her goal but she was only going to stay in the police for ten years. She was thrilled to bits her dream would come true and happy to know her dad was around her. He had been killed in a work accident many years before. I heard a few months later that she had successfully passed her entrance exams and was now a fully-fledged officer. However, it didn't end there. Many years later, approximately twelve years on, my sister Eileen ran into Joan whilst out shopping. Joan was buying toiletries and nightwear and Eileen asked if she was going on holiday. Joan said, "I wish." She was actually shopping to prepare to go into a hospice. Joan told Eileen she had terminal cancer and was going there to die. She asked how I was and told Eileen I had been right; she had served as a police officer for ten years before becoming ill and had to leave on health grounds. Eileen and I went to visit Joan in the hospice; unfortunately, she was too ill to receive visitors that day, so we left flowers for her and left. Sadly, Joan passed over a few weeks later.

By now it was June 1994. I received my results from university, and I had passed the second year of my degree with flying colours.

By October, my attendance at church had started to dwindle and I wasn't attending as much as I would have liked. This wasn't because I didn't want to, I just didn't have the time. It was the third and final year of my degree and I was on for a good classification if I put the work in. I spent every spare minute studying, writing assignments and preparing for exams. If I wanted to do well, there was no cutting corners. I needed to give it one hundred percent. I was still working and doing readings too, however, I had so many people trying to book appointments I had to start spreading them out as word about the accuracy of my messages had spread far and wide. The people I read for came from all walks of life. I read for people who had lost children, for some who had lost loved ones to suicide and a lot of times for those who were having relationship problems.

Life was ultra-busy, and I was running round like a headless chicken trying to manage all the things I needed to do. I wasn't sleeping particularly well either.

I drove to university one day and parked in the same place I did every day I went there. When I returned later to go home, the car had gone; it had been stolen. This was the straw that broke the camel's back. Now I had to sort this out too, contacting the police and insurance was all time-consuming and time I didn't have. I still had a thousand words left to write for an assignment that needed to be submitted the next day!

It was later that night I suffered my first ever panic attack. My mouth went dry, my heart was pounding, and I felt that I couldn't breathe. I had never experienced anything like it, I thought I was having a heart attack. I was blue lighted to hospital by ambulance and landed up having an ECG to check my heart. The doctor assured me I was physically fine and the reason I had had these symptoms was probably due to a panic attack brought on by stress. I rang my tutor the next day and was given a couple of days grace to submit my outstanding work.

I went to meditate and speak to my guide. Savanna said I needed to slow down and stop doing so much. I knew something had to give but I didn't know what. Everything I did was important. I needed to work for the income, I needed to study to gain my degree and I didn't really want to give up doing readings because I loved helping people. I called out to Glyn in the spirit world and asked him to help me. As the weeks went by I stopped attending church and the demand for readings seemed to reduce too. I felt the spirit world was giving me a rest so I could just concentrate for now on work and study.

The panic attack had left me anxious, and I started to worry about everything. Did Gary still love me? Was I going to fail my degree? Had I made a good enough job of raising Nicola? The thoughts went on and on. Despite the anxiety, I was able to finish my degree. On results day, I had arranged to meet Cath so we could go and look at the classification results together following the exam board. I already knew I had passed but my marks were borderline between two classifications. I wouldn't know my final results until they had been posted on the noticeboard. We sipped coffee and waited in anticipation for the marks to be posted. Eventually an administrator appeared and pinned the results on the board. Cath found her results almost immediately; she had done really well. It took me a while to find my name on the long list, I was looking in the 2.1 section and couldn't see my name. I thought I will start at the top where the first-class honours were published and work my way down top to bottom until I found my results. I got to the third name down and there it was. Not only had I passed, but I had also been awarded a first-class degree with honours. To say I was over the moon was an understatement. Just five people from our class were awarded a first that year and I was one of them. I immediately thanked my spirit family and friends in the spirit world in my mind. I knew they had pushed me on to the finish. I rang Gary with my news and later that night we celebrated with a nice cool bottle of champagne.

As graduation day approached, I couldn't stop thinking about Ruth. I thought how sad she wouldn't be here to collect her degree. She was always very bright, and I know she would have done really well had she been given the time to finish her studies. Cath and I went to see the head of department and asked if they could award Ruth a degree in her memory. The head said that wasn't possible, but they would have a look at the work she had already done before she became ill and see if she qualified for some sort of award. At graduation later that summer Cath and I were presented with our degree certificates and Ruth was awarded a certificate in higher education. When the vice chancellor read out Ruth's name, I stood up and started clapping loudly. Soon the whole room were up on their feet and applauding her too. Ruth has stayed close to my heart ever since and I know she has helped me from beyond the grave many times since.

# Chapter 4
## Helping others

Now I had my degree I turned to thinking about my future career. I had thought for a long time I would like to be a social worker as I would be helping lots of people just as Janine had said I would all those years ago. In order to make this a reality, I would need a postgraduate degree in social work. I applied to Manchester University. I was called in for an interview and to take an entrance exam.

I flew through the exam in the morning and was called in for the interview in the afternoon. I entered the room and was greeted by two social work lecturers. They said I had passed the entrance exam and now they wanted to know more about me. They set me scenarios and asked how I would deal with the problems they presented. They moved on to ask me about myself, what work I had done and my interests. When I got to explaining my interests, I started to tell them about my spiritual work. I was never ashamed of being a medium, it was part of who I was, and I wasn't going to hide it now. I looked up at one of the lecturers and I could see her rolling her eyes in the back of her head. I knew in that moment they thought I was unhinged or something and I wouldn't get a place.

As sure as eggs are eggs a letter arrived a few days later saying I had not been accepted onto the course. I was upset but also knew it wasn't meant to be for a reason. That reason was revealed a couple of years later. In the second paragraph in my rejection letter, it said there were places still available for the Master of Arts degree in social policy. I had studied quite a bit of social policy as part of my undergraduate degree and really enjoyed it. I thought, what the heck, I'll pop an application in.

It was September 1995 when I arrived at Manchester University to start my postgraduate master's degree. I met some really interesting people and made friends with a lady called Julie. She was doing the course part-time as her day job was as the Chief Executive of a large hospital. One day whilst chatting to Julie I could see her aura; rather than being bright and vibrant, it displayed patches of grey, I knew this wasn't right and there was trouble around her. A few weeks later a scandal broke at the hospital where she was in charge. It was nothing to do with her personally but, given her position, she was scapegoated and forced to resign. I never saw her again, but I wished her well. It just showed what having a top profile job can do to you. Around this time, there were also a number of cases in the media reporting how social services had let down a number of children who had been murdered by their parents. I thought, thank God I was stopped from going down the social work route. This was one of many examples throughout my life when spirit had stepped in to stop me doing the wrong thing.

By summer 1996, I had completed my master's degree and graduated with a distinction for research. I was now thirty-five years old and was still working part-time as a waitress. Time to evaluate and work out where I was heading next. I meditated as I often did. Turning to Savanna and my spirit family and friends, I asked for some guidance. The answer I got back was quite surprising. I was told I should stay in education! By now I had been studying in full-time higher education for almost five years, could I really justify doing more?

I had always dreamed of doing a PhD, but could I really warrant doing another three years of full-time study? Fortunately, Gary was earning quite good money by now and my mother was so proud of what I had achieved and wanted me to further achieve, she once again offered to help me with the fees. By September I was signed up to start a PhD. I was allocated two prominent professors to supervise my research. Both were experts in health policy, and it was in this field I decided to undertake my studies. I wrote a couple of very long essays on the subject and was assured I was on the right track which was reassuring. I was enjoying my studies but sometimes it could be lonely, unlike the last five years, studying was now an individual pursuit, and I didn't have any classmates for camaraderie.

A few months into my PhD studies I was reading a newspaper when I 'stumbled' across a part-time hourly paid lecturing post at another local university. I could hear Savanna's voice in my head telling me to apply. I thought I would have no chance as I had never taught in my life. However, I did what I was guided to do and put an application form in.

A couple of weeks later I got a phone call from the head of the social work department at the University of Salford asking me to come in for an interview. The day of my interview arrived, I put on my best suit and off I went. On the train journey there I asked myself, what the hell was I doing, I have no teaching experience as such. I had given a few presentations as a student but never been paid to do it. With that familiar knot in my stomach, I knocked on the head's door. Sitting there was the head of social work and the head of social policy. Both were really nice to me and soon I was feeling at ease. They said they were looking for someone to teach a history of social policy module to social work students as one of the lecturers had gone off on long-term sick leave. They asked if I could do it. I explained I had studied this subject at undergraduate and postgraduate level for over five years. They had my CV and application form in front of them so could see the level of qualifications I had. They asked me a few more questions about my knowledge of the subject, and the interview was over. Doug, the head of department, said he would be in touch. I wasn't sure how it had gone but

I had answered all the questions presented to me and now, with little hope, I just had to wait. Later that evening the phone rang. It was Doug, the Head of Department who had interviewed me. I thought, that was quick, he was probably just giving me a courtesy call to say I had not been successful. No such thing. He said they had been impressed with me and he wanted to offer me the post. I was gobsmacked. Of course, I said yes, and within a couple of weeks I was standing in a classroom lecturing. I absolutely loved it. The satisfaction I got from helping the students was just fantastic.

A few weeks into my teaching, I was lecturing away when I noticed a light getting stronger at the back of the room, Janine, my friend from school who had passed following the motorbike accident, was standing there as clear as day. She said I was now helping people in the way that I should, just as she had said I would do when she first visited me from the spirit world all those years ago. I carried on lecturing with the assurance I had finally found my place in the world and was exactly where I was meant to be. I finally finished working at the restaurant and put all my energy into teaching and my PhD.

A few weeks later I was chatting with Stephen, the head of the social policy programmes, when he asked me what other social policy related modules I could teach. I rambled off a list of the topics I was interested in and had some knowledge of. Amongst these were health policy and gender studies. He was immediately interested and asked if I could write a health policy module and teach it as this was something missing from the undergraduate curriculum on the social policy degree. A week or so later I took my module plan to Stephen to look over. He was pleased with it, and we presented it to the module approval board. Within weeks it was passed and from the start of the next semester I was also teaching health policy to third year students. Every week I was asked to take on more; the supervision of student dissertations, personal tutoring, teaching gender issues and attending staff meetings and exam boards.

Before I knew it, I was almost full time. I loved every minute of it, but I was still being paid an hourly rate and didn't have a permanent contract. I went to see Doug, the Head of Department, who said, 'he would see what he could do'. Sometime later I received a letter from human resources saying I was being offered an annual contract. This meant I would have a proper contract for twelve months with a proper salary to go with it. I just knew my spirit family had guided this to happen for me. Of course, I accepted and soon I was as familiar as a piece of furniture in the department. I was always at work, giving it one hundred percent. This was all fantastic and I couldn't believe I was now a fully-fledged lecturer. This was all fine, but my PhD began to suffer; I no longer had the time for it the way I had. As my twelve-month contract at work was coming to an end, I once again went to see the head of department. I asked Doug if my contract was going to be renewed? He said this wasn't possible as they were only allowed to keep people on yearly contracts for one year. If I was to stay on, I would have to get a permanent position. My heart sank. I thought this journey was going to end. Doug said he was pleased with the work I had done and once again he said, "Let me see what I can do, we really don't want to lose you if we can help it." A few weeks later I was called in for another interview and had to give a presentation to the other staff members on what I could bring to the department if I was given a permanent position. I worked for days and days on my presentation, brainstorming ideas and writing out the things I could do for the department and the students if I was given the opportunity.

Interview day arrived and I was that nervous I was nearly on the verge of another panic attack. My whole future hinged on this day, and I hadn't a clue what I would do if I didn't get a post. On the train ride to the university, I sent a thought out to Savanna and my spirit family asking for their help to calm me down. As I stepped off the train, I saw a gold star on the floor; it was like one of those you used to get on your school work when you had done well. I knew straight away Savanna had sent this for me and by the time I entered the interview and presentation room, I just knew it would go well. A few days later I received a letter. I had been offered a permanent part-time position. All of my hard work had paid off, I now had a career I loved and a regular income to boot. I thanked the spirit world again because I knew they had had a hand in helping me to get to this place on my journey.

It wasn't long before my contract was amended, and I was working full time. Life was busy and I was still doing psychic readings in my spare time. I tried to separate the day job from my spiritual work. I was doing readings in the evenings and teaching social policy by day. As with all things where there's a high, there is always a low. My PhD had sat on my desk untouched now for several months. It wasn't that I didn't want to do it, I just couldn't find the time. My anxiety had returned through worrying about it and something had to give before I did. I couldn't give up the day job and I didn't want to stop my psychic work, I owed this to the spirit world. I went to see my PhD supervisor and explained my plight. I was told not to beat myself up about it. If I already had a permanent job in academia, the PhD wasn't that important at this moment. After all, I already had a postgraduate degree. With a heavy heart, I suspended my studies with the intent to pick it up again later when life wasn't so hectic. In effect, it was another twenty-eight years later before I looked at it again once I retired. Even without the PhD I got involved with undertaking research, writing articles and contributing to text books. My work was even published in the prestigious *British Medical Journal* too.

Gary had suffered from migraines for years, one night I got an overwhelming feeling I should put my hands on his head. I had heard and seen people doing spiritual healing, but it was something I had never trained in or tried. As I placed my hand on his forehead, I could fell a warm glow building around my hands and I just knew intuitively it was spirit who was guiding this. Within minutes Gary was feeling much better and slept like a baby that night. I was fascinated by this phenomenon; I had never felt the power of spiritual healing before. A while after meditating, a spirit person came close to my aura. He appeared as an elderly man with receding hair. He later told me his name was Bert and he would be working with me in the future as my healing guide.

I went on to practice this new gift on friends and family. By running my hands a few inches from the body, I could feel where people's health problems were; in the back, in the legs, the head, etcetera. With practice, I began to see people's auras much clearer and could pinpoint illness this way too. Illness was usually located in the site where the aura was dark or torn. Eventually I added this service to my readings. I learned healing the aura, usually helped to heal the body too. With Bert guiding me, I went on to help hundreds of people, and still do to this day.

# Chapter 5
## An improvement in development

By the 1990s, my dad was living in a care home. He had
Parkinson's disease and dementia. Dad lived with my
sister for the previous few years. She did an excellent
job of looking after him, but his behaviour had seriously
deteriorated. He would get up in the middle of the night
and switch the gas on the cooker without lighting it. My
sister still had children living at home and it had become
unsafe. I went to visit my dad but hated it; it was so sad
to see him this way.

It was the fourth of April 2002, and I was due to fly
to Portugal on the sixth for a much-needed break. I
thought I would call in to see my dad before I went. This
day he looked so much better than I had seen him for
some time, he had had his hair cut and was looking
smart and relaxed. There was a feeling of serenity
around him. I laughed and joked with him saying I
would bring a nice Portuguese lady back with me to
keep him company. A few hours later I got a phone call
to tell me Dad had passed over in his sleep. I was sad
but also happy for him; he no longer had to face the
torment that had plagued him, he was free. I cancelled

the holiday and began to help with the funeral arrangements.

Not long after Dad's funeral someone mentioned they were going to a psychic supper later that week. Immediately my ears pricked up and I asked if I could go too. The following Friday I found myself sitting with about twenty other people in a café called Coffee and Crystals. The medium who was hosting the evening was called Julie and I took to her straight away. It felt like I had known her for a long time, but that night was actually the first time I had met her. I had a pleasant evening; she had us drawing pictures, swapping them over with others and got us see what we could get from the picture psychically. After supper Julie did a demonstration of mediumship and I got a message from the spirit world from my dad. I was so pleased he was now at peace. As the evening came to a close, I was speaking with Julie when she told me she ran development classes, and I would be welcome to attend. I hadn't sat in a development group since I had sat in the spiritual church circle some years before.

The following Sunday, I found myself back at Julie's café but this day it wasn't open to the public and was being used as a spiritual space. When I arrived, there were already about a dozen people sitting in a circle waiting to start. Lovely pan pipe music was playing in the background and the atmosphere felt really calm. We meditated, did various exercises to strengthen our mediumship and sent out healing to the world. I had a wonderful day and stayed in development with Julie and my peers for the next four years until the shop was sold and Julie moved on. I formed some very strong friendships with some of the others I sat with, Carol, Marion, Karen and Tracey, amongst others. Whilst giving Tracey a reading one day I said I could see her writing a book in the future. Since then, she has written and published three books on spiritualism, angels and mindfulness.

With no development class to go to any more, I returned to my old spiritualist church and religiously sat in the Wednesday night open circle. There were people at all different levels of their spiritual journey. some just stepping onto their spiritual path, others had been mediums for years. We all encouraged each other with giving spirit messages and it was always a pleasant night. I would feel calm and relaxed after each circle and this helped me keep focused at work too. Occasionally I was asked to take the Sunday divine service and was always happy to oblige.

In 2010, I decided to change my religion from Church of England to that of spiritualist. It made more sense to me now and my daughter decided to join me too. We had a lovely naming ceremony and were finally ordained as a fully-fledged spiritualists. I continued sitting in the open circle for the next couple of years. Within the space of a few months, however, the atmosphere changed. Some of the group, were bickering and fighting for popularity. The whole ambience of the place changed. What I was witnessing was as far from spiritualism as you could get; some had let their egos get the better of them. One day, I was talking to Carol from Julie's development class when she told me she and Marion had been visiting a different spiritualist church. She said it was a lovely place and I should come along and try it. The following Sunday I arrived at the said spiritual church for the divine service. It wasn't long before I was fully integrated there, and people found out I was a practicing medium. The church booking secretary asked if she could book me to take a service. I did several services after that at that church, and it provided me with the opportunity to demonstrate my mediumship and to pass on messages to those in need from their loved ones in the spirit world.

I was glad my dad had found peace at last from his tormented life. He had never been himself for years, not since the night of his accident. Although I was happy he was now at peace, I still grieved for him. His death stirred up a lot of memories for me and they weren't all good ones. I started to feel guilty about not doing more for Dad and wondering if Glyn would still be here if I had taken him in when he was unwell? I was really beating myself up. My anxiety returned and one day, when running late from a meeting to teach, panic struck, and I started having a massive anxiety attack. I locked myself in a toilet cubicle and stayed there till the attack subsided. I went into the class late and apologised to the students saying I had been held up. Somehow, I got through the lecture, but as soon as I could afterwards, I grabbed my coat and went home.

The panic attack had frightened me so much. I was so scared of it happening again I went off sick from work and didn't leave the house for another six months! Eventually, I slowly starting going out again, at first with Gary by my side and later on my own. In due course, I returned to work and tried to put the whole sorry incident behind me. Before long, things were back to normal, work was going well, and I had started doing readings and attending church again. Life went on as normal, the agoraphobia I had suffered left me with anxiety but, if I didn't overdo it, it was manageable. I had seen a couple of doctors about it but didn't really get much help from them. I was prescribed beta blockers and left to get on with it.

Another five years or so passed without incident, and by then I had been promoted three times. Firstly, I became the programme leader, then an associate director followed by a rise to senior lectureship. Everything was swinging along; I had a dedicated staff group working with me and the students who came and went were happy with the service they received. By then, I had called on one of our star ex-students to help out with seminars and she made such a good impression it wasn't long before she was integrated into the team with a permanent contract. I had always admired Karen; she had a son with severe autism to care for and still managed to get a first-class honours degree when she had previously studied on the programme I taught. We became great friends as well as colleagues and she has been my rock on many occasions. We were only a small team and had more than a healthy share of students to teach but we all got stuck in and did our best.

One day, around 2010, we were told the department was to appoint a new professor. My colleagues and I didn't get a say in the selection of the candidate; this was decided higher up the chain. Our new colleague joined us around October 2010. At first, he was quite charming, and we were all in awe of how much research he had done. He joined our team but soon made it clear he would be doing little teaching as he had research projects to see to and apply for. We could have done with another hands-on lecturer to take some of the strain off the other staff, including me. Alas, we took it on the chin and ploughed on. After a while, the said professor started to be derogatory to myself and other staff. He tried to belittle some of us and said it was disappointing how little research we had notched up in comparison to him. He would get quite vicious in staff meetings sometimes and was upsetting the status quo. I tried to explain to him, that other members of staff weren't able to do the level of research we would like, due to the heavy teaching load. He wasn't impressed and morale within the team soon disintegrated. I tried my best to ignore him, but stress started to get the better of me. He got really cross in a meeting one day. He was bright red in the face, and I thought he was going to give himself a heart attack. I had to tell him to calm down.

I'm not saying it was his fault, but it was the straw that broke the camel's back, and not long after this incident the panic attacks returned with a vengeance. I was scared to leave the house again and ended up signed off work for the best part of a year. I was devastated that this had happened to me again. Whilst at home, I had plenty of time to think about my life and the things that had happened to me in the past. I came to the conclusion that I had bottled a lot of things up that hadn't been dealt with. With spiritual healing and therapy, I learned to deal with my pent-up emotions and how to let them go.

By 2011, I was back at work feeling stronger than ever; teaching and doing research too. After a couple of years, the said professor moved on and was replaced by another professor who was really amenable and helpful. Life went on and I even found time to contribute to writing a text book. By now I had become very mindful of not taking too much on. I had always been a yes person, willing to take on everyone else's problems and demands. To avoid being ill again I had to learn to say no. I rearranged my work and home life to a more manageable level. Throughout this time, I still followed my spiritual practice, meditating most days and spending times with my spirit guides. As an effect of this, my mediumship and healing ability grew even stronger. They say all the best mediums have overcome adversity in their lives; well, I had certainly done that.

I returned to the church development circle with Marion and Carol and enjoyed every minute of it. My energy had become so sensitive I could pick up on other people's emotions and illnesses. This was all well and good except I was sometimes taking on these emotions and feelings myself and it could be quite overwhelming. I was soon guided by Bert to carry out a protection ritual each day to block out the problems of others. I learned how to switch my psychic gift on and off and this was really convenient.

I continued to do one-to-one readings and got some fantastic results for my sitters. Spirits were coming through thick and fast, and it was an honour to be the medium between this world and the next. Mothers, brothers, sisters, fathers and friends would relay messages through me and sometimes the recipients were overjoyed that they had had contact with their departed loved ones. One lady who came to see me was having great difficulty walking and was using crutches. After her sitting I offered to do some spiritual healing on her. She agreed. I placed my hands a couple of inches from her body and tuned into her aura. I could soon feel and see in her aura that the problem causing her poor walking wasn't coming from her legs but from her lower back. The aura in this area of her body was dull and torn. I immediately placed my hands and focus on her back. The warmth coming through my hands was immense. I took the spiritual thread from the spirit world that Bert was passing to me and stitched the aura where it was torn. I went on to work on a couple of more places on her aura that looked dull and then asked her to stand up. She was up and out of the chair without support and her aura was looking so much brighter. I explained what I had done and showed her where her problem was coming from. I would never try to take the place of a medical doctor and I feel my healing is complementary. I advised her to see her GP and tell them she had a slipped disc. A few days later I got a phone call from her telling me she was managing to walk round her house without crutches and she felt like it was a miracle as she had been on crutches for a couple of years. I have had many results like this, but I don't take the credit, I am only the vessel used by the spirit world to bring about this phenomenon.

Not only did the spirit world carry out physical healing through me, it has also helped with people's mental health too. People who have been depressed for years have become lighter and brighter in front of my very eyes. One young man's healing session in particular stands out. This young man was about nineteen and had been badly bullied at school. He had started life as a girl and was undergoing gender augmentation. He had been ridiculed for being different throughout all his teenage years. As I ran my hands round his aura, I could feel his sadness haemorrhaging from him. I could have wept for him. Not only had the bullies knocked the fight out of him mentally, they had also impacted his aura; it was one of the dullest I have ever seen. As I started running my hands round his aura he began to sob. I could see all the repressed emotions leaving him. At the end of the session, I could physically see the change in him. He looked so much brighter and even gave me a smile. Not happy that just one session was enough to deal with such a deep-seated issue, I suggested he continued to see me for a few more times. After five weeks of regular attendance, the frightened depressed young person who had come through my door left much happier and confident. I understand he had a full sex change in his twenties and is now living a fulfilling life helping other young people to overcome adversity. If the spirit world and I have played just a small part in bringing about this positive change, I am thankful.

# Chapter 6
## Teaching for spirit

Gary and I had enjoyed the first home we bought together so much we stayed there for nearly twenty-five years. Our garden was second to none and we had a large allotment at the back of the garden where we grew lots of fruit and veg. Alas, as many places do, the area we lived in started to change. Many of the neighbours had grown old and passed over whilst we were there and some of the younger ones moving in didn't have the same pride in their properties or gardens like the previous owners had. Our immediate neighbour Kathleen passed in her nineties; she was a wonderful person and we treated her like family. After she had gone, another family moved in. Without planning permission, they built a large extension that overlooked what was then my private garden. Our privacy was shattered. Every time we went outside one of them would be standing at the back door smoking and staring into our garden. We are by no means antisocial, but we really missed what used to be our private space, especially in the summer when we wanted to sunbathe. We decided to sell up and move on. We searched high and low for the right property to no avail.

One evening, a couple of months later, Gary asked what I thought of a house he showed me a picture of on the internet. I was immediately smitten. It was an old nineteenth-century gatehouse, set in a tree-lined road, which had once belonged to the mansion of a wealthy cotton merchant. We contacted the estate agent and tried to make an appointment. It became problematic as they said they were having difficulty contacting the vendor in order to make a viewing appointment. A few weeks passed and we still hadn't viewed the property. I had my heart set on it so took matters into my own hands. I wrote a letter outlining our interest and posted it through the owner's door asking him to phone me. A few more weeks had passed when the phone call came. The vendor apologised, explaining he had recently lost his mother and his focus had been there. This was perfectly understandable and within the week he invited us round to have a look. The lodge, as it was called, was very rundown and needed a lot of work, but the atmosphere of the place was, however, electric. The basement room was big, and I immediately saw its potential as a spiritual centre. We agreed a price and within weeks we were the proud owners of Knowsley Grange Lodge.

At this stage, it was hardly habitable, so we rented a house on a short lease and set about renovating the lodge. Within six months we moved in. The renovation made such a big difference. The house was immaculate, and the renovation really brought it to life. I decked the basement out with spiritual trinkets and was soon using it for doing readings. I loved this space, and it had a wonderful atmosphere. Sometimes I would see the spirit of people who had previously lived there. I got to learn a lot about the past life of one of them in particular. Anne had been in service in the mansion house and shared this property with others who also worked for the cotton merchant. Life was harsh for a lot of people then; there was much poverty and a plague to contend with. Who said history doesn't repeat itself?

Around the same time as moving, I was asked to lead the development group at the local spiritualist church. The aim was to help others bring out their mediumistic gift. Janine hadn't been joking all those years ago when she told me I was destined to help people; I was now teaching day and night and loving every minute of it. Each week I would set the development students exercises to bring out their mediumistic and psychic skills. The word spread and the group grew from strength to strength; at one stage, over sixty people a week attended. The church took a small charge from attendees in order to contribute to the upkeep of the church. The committee offered to pay me a fee which had been the case in the past for others. I declined to be paid; I was working for spirit, and you couldn't put a price on that. I met some fabulous people through doing this class and it was a pleasure to watch them blossom spiritually. We did a lot of meditation, practicing meeting our guides and giving messages. We also had some social events where we would meet up and go out to dinner.

One of the group's members, let's call her Sharon, told me one evening she was pregnant. I congratulated her and said I hope all went well. A few weeks later I thought Sharon didn't look herself and I knew intuitively something was wrong. Speaking to Sharon later, she told me she had been having some tests, which revealed the baby had a congenital condition and would be born with disabilities. The doctors told her if the baby survived birth, it would be living with a life-limiting condition. I was devastated for Sharon and wanted to do something to help. Her son M was born alive, and, unlike other children, he could not feed normally and was to be permanently fed through a tube. With both this situation and other disabilities Sharon did a grand job of looking after him. My sister Eileen and myself went to see him and what a beautiful baby he was. I asked the chair of the church committee if we could have a psychic supper to raise some money to help Sharon and the baby. Obviously, Sharon couldn't work as baby M needed care. The chair said this was a good idea and she would run it by the committee at their next meeting.

That night I posted on my Facebook page to advertise the up-and-coming event. Although I didn't have a definite date yet, I thought I would try and drum up some interest. Lots of people showed interest and I was looking forward to the said night.

A few days later I received a phone call asking me to go in to see the church committee. I assumed they were going to set a date for the up-and-coming fund raiser, but how wrong could I have been! I entered the meeting and was greeted with a room of glum faces. I said hello and sat down. I asked if they had now got a date in place for the upcoming psychic supper? The chair, who had originally said it was a good idea, said it wouldn't be happening and she never had said it could. I was gobsmacked. Another member of the committee had been standing there when she had originally said it was a good idea. I looked to this committee member for support, but they said they couldn't remember what had been said. I couldn't believe what I was hearing. The committee continued to speak to me like I was a naughty six-year-old, telling me I had no right putting it on Facebook. I sat and listened to them a little longer before reminding them I had brought thousands of pounds into the church through running the development class and it was only fair they let me have the fundraiser. I asked for their rationale for refusing the event but not one of them came back with a reasonable answer. I thought, have these people remembered they are supposed to be running a spiritualist church because from where I was sitting there was nothing spiritual about their behaviour at all? I had heard enough. I asked to be excused, picked my bag up and left in disgust. I later found out the underlying cause for all this bad behaviour stemmed from jealousy.

Once I left the church that night I didn't return again for years. I now had my own spiritual place, and I was going to utilise it. I contacted as many of the people I had taught in the church development class and said I would be running the group from my home in the future, and many of them followed me there. The spirit had worked miracles again, giving me the space required to continue my spiritual work. I hosted the psychic supper for Sharon at my home. It was a successful evening and substantial funds were raised. Some of my medium friends gave their time to give free readings. Good intentions always win out and Sharon and her family bought some sensory equipment for the baby and took a much-needed short break with the rest of the money raised. Sadly, baby M died just before his second birthday and my sister, and I attended the funeral. Sometime later I was able to pass a spirit message onto his mum. She said she now felt better knowing he was safe and being cared for in the spirit world. I felt privileged to have known baby M and was glad I had been able to make a difference in his short life on earth however small that was. Gary and I bought an apple tree in baby M's memory, and it continues to grow in his mum's garden to this day and Sharon and I have stayed friends. It was definitely time to move on from that church and I knew once again spirit had a hand in it. They had led me to a new space in my home to assist me in continuing my work for them. The spirit always leads us to the right place, for the right reasons.

# Chapter 7
## The home circle

By now it was 2014. I continued in my day job and ran spiritual awareness and development classes in the evening from home. I was lucky to have the space to run my classes. I did, and still do, awareness classes to help those who are new to their spiritual journey. I usually limit numbers to a manageable level so everyone can get some one-to-one time with me after class. Awareness classes usually last for eight weeks. I have had some lovely groups to work with over the years.

The course starts with teaching how to meditate. It is important if you are going to be a good medium that you learn to clear space in your mind to allow spirit to work through your faculties. Secondly, students learn how to feel their spirit guide around them. My calling card is that I can feel a fluttering sensation around my chin. Different people have different calling cards; some get hot, some feel someone stroking their hair and others may get butterflies in the stomach. It doesn't matter how you know spirit is around you, it's just important to know when your guide is there. Your guide is the gatekeeper to the spirit world and will help you communicate messages between the spirit world and the sitter. This exercise is important for all trainee mediums. I believe mediumship is a gift but if you are going to be good at it, like anything in life, it takes practice and that's what spiritual awareness is all about.

Each week we would do a different exercise, such as learning to see the aura as this can tell you a lot about the person you are reading for. We would learn how to do psychometry, which is how to do a reading by holding an object that belonged to a departed spirit. There is a brief overview of spiritualism and the mediums who have gone before. I would give the group photos of deceased people they didn't know and see what information they could get from the photos; this is a good way of stretching the psyche and being able to pick up on the characteristics and traits of spirit under question. Towards the end of the course, I get students to give messages to each other from spirit with the assistance of their guide. I have witnessed some wonderful messages and descriptions of the sitters' loved ones in the spirit world. However, as I always tell the students, you don't become a proficient medium overnight. It takes time and dedication to get to a reasonable standard. Students who do well in awareness class move into the spiritual development circle. Those who decide it's not for them step off and those still not confident enough to step up to development take extra tutorials and practice until they feel confident. As I tell all the students, it is not a race or a competition, we all bloom in our own time.

All the students coming into the development circle have already done their awareness training and are dedicated to serving the spirit world in their quest to communicate with loved ones here on earth. All humans and animals are made from energy. It's the law of physics and when the physical body dies the energy lives on; this is sometimes referred to as the soul or the spirit. This energy vibrates at a higher frequency than that of the human body. Becoming a medium is all about been able to change your energy to meet this higher frequency. This takes years to perfect and even some of the world's most well-known mediums continue to sit in a development circle for their whole life trying to perfect this skill. The better one becomes at meeting spirit frequency the better and clearer the messages become. I have some people who have sat in my circle on a weekly basis since it began over ten years ago. As well as practicing our mediumistic skills, we often send healing out to each other and the wider world in general. Spirits are fantastic at leading the right people to the right place at the right time and everyone in the circle has been brought together for the common goal of supporting each other and improving their mediumship. Different circle participants use different faculties to receive messages from the spirit world. Some can see spirit (this is called clairvoyance), some can hear them (clairaudience), and some can feel or smell them (clairsentients). Some work with a mixture of all these faculties. I, for example, am very clairsentient but spirit often use my other faculties to make me aware they are there.

One particular Thursday night arrived, and the members of the home circle started to arrive. That night a lady who had completed the awareness class joined us. As I always do, I led a guided meditation to get the group relaxed and tuned in to their spirit guides. As I was doing the meditation, I was drawn to our new member, let's call her Sue to protect her privacy. Her aura looked dull, and I could feel an air of grief around her. We went round the group taking turns to give messages. When it was my turn, I was very much drawn to Sue. I could see the outline of a young fair-haired man standing behind her. I instinctively knew it was her son. I could feel a tightening around my neck and just knew he had passed through hanging. He said he was glad his mum was wearing his necklace as this would always keep them close. He apologised for leaving the world the way he had but assured her he was now fine and had met up with his father in the spirit world. The relief for Sue, hearing from her son, was amazing. She had apparently been visiting mediums hoping for a message for years but until now she had none. Her aura immediately started to become lighter and brighter, and she was overwhelmed that she had finally heard from her son. The peace on her face was priceless.

We have had many experiences like this over the years. I too have received many accurate messages from the spirit world through circle participants. One such message was delivered to me through Bob, who described a lady that I could recognise as my mother-in-law, June. He told me she had passed over with cancer which was true. June assured me that she was now well and sent love to Gary and all the family. Bob said she was also showing him a piece of jewellery and described a brooch to me. I later went and got the brooch he had described from June's jewellery box that had sat in a bedroom drawer since she passed. I showed it to the group, and it was exactly like Bob had described it. It was such evidence that proved beyond doubt that life after death goes on. Before this Bob hadn't known my mother-in-law had passed and he certainly didn't know I had the brooch he had described in my possession. We have had thousands of messages from beyond the veil over the years, all of them unique and personal to the recipient.

In addition to passing messages on to each other I sometimes give the group exercises to do. One of the most popular ones is being a psychic detective. I give the group a picture of a person who passed in inauspicious circumstances, someone who has been murdered or passed in a tragic way, for example. I ask them to study the picture and tune into the person in the photograph and try to get as much information as possible about what led to the end of their bodily experience on earth. The group have often got excellent information using this method. One day I gave them a picture of a lady that no one in the group knew anything about who had sadly been murdered by her ex-partner. I, of course, had the back story to the circumstances that had taken her life. The lady in question had been a nurse who was stabbed to death in the street by her jealous ex-partner. Working in pairs, the group discussed the photo and wrote down everything they felt about it. The results are often outstanding as they were in this case. When the pairs fed back to the main group, the information when pulled together was solid. Between the group, they had got the name of the lady in question, the name of her perpetrator, information about her family, the way she had been killed and a good overview of the type of work she had done prior to her death.

As well as using clairvoyance to communicate with spirit, I sometimes teach other methods. For example, by scrying, that's looking into a candle flame. It is possible by using this method to see signs and symbols, sometimes images of faces or words and initials. All this information can be pulled together into a message. Psychometry is also a different way of collecting information from the deceased. By holding an object that belonged to a person who has passed over it is possible to pick up on their vibration and the imprint of the energy they have left behind. This method is usually most successful when using personal items such as jewellery. Although reading tarot, angel or playing cards in readings is much disputed by some mediums, I argue that by doing this you can bring extra strength to the reading. I'm not suggesting you learn how to read cards from a book, although this is perfectly okay if that's what you would like to do. I suggest you look at the cards and use your intuition to interpret what the pictures and symbols are saying to you. In my experience, sitters are glad to hear from their loved ones in the spirit world but most of them also want to know what is going on in their life and what is coming in their future. If using cards to do this is useful, then why not? The more a sitter gets from a psychic/mediumistic reading, the happier and more satisfied they are.

After development class one evening, one of the group, Arthur, said he had recently moved to an old farmhouse in the countryside. He said he was aware of a presence around the property and asked us if we would like to go over for supper one evening so he could get our view? The appointed evening arrived and my sister Eileen, who had sat in the circle from the start, and I drove over to the farmhouse. When we arrived, we noticed an old Victorian-looking barn to the right and a quaint farmhouse to the left. It was around Christmas time and the house was quite high up; as you looked back over the distant town, you could see the fairy lights on the houses twinkling. It began to snow, and all looked really pretty and seasonal. We entered the front door to see other members of the circle waiting for us. As I stepped over the threshold, I could feel the atmosphere drop; there was an unusual heaviness in the air. We all greeted each other, then the host took us on a tour of the house and surrounding area. As I walked by the barn, I began to shiver. I wasn't sure at this time why I felt so uneasy, but I was soon about to find out. We had supper then settled down to discuss if anyone had picked anything up. Everyone agreed there was something not right here but none of us could pinpoint what it was.

We decided to have a séance to see if this would shed some light on it. We set the table up like a Ouija board using letters and numbers and yes and no cards. We used an upturned glass as the planchet and off we went. No sooner had we put our fingers on the glass, than it started to move vigorously. We asked who was there and immediately the glass moved around the board spelling out a name. We established it was a male spirit we were conversing with, and his name was Bob. We began to ask Bob questions and he continued to answer by spelling out more words. The atmosphere got even heavier, and the light started to flicker, I can't say we were frightened but we were all highly vigilant. I began to get a sharp pain across my forehead and my vision began to blur. I knew a spirit was trying to overshadow me and a vision of Bob's features began to build. I spoke to him and asked what it was he wanted. As clear as a bell, he shouted, "Help." We took our fingers off the glass, and I called on one of my guides for advice. Savanna told me Bob's soul was stuck between the earth plane and the spirit world. I asked her what we should do. She said we should pray and ask his guide to take him to the light. Bob, the poor soul, had been stuck in limbo. We lit a candle for Bob, said a prayer and called out to his loved ones in the spirit world to come and collect him. As we drove home that night it was snowing heavily but the atmosphere felt much lighter.

The next time I saw Arthur he said the house felt a lot better and there had been no sightings of Bob or anything untoward since. Some years later I heard a tale that a young man called Robert had shot himself in the head after his wife left him. That certainly explained why I had had such a bad headache that night.

Sometimes at the development circle we also have visiting mediums come along to give demonstrations of mediumship. One particular evening we had invited a trance medium called Colin. We all got comfy and waited for the demonstration to begin. Colin went into a deep level of relaxation, when he began to speak it was his guides voice, not Colin's, who spoke to us. He gave us his philosophy on life then started to go round the room giving each one of us a message. When he got to me, he told me there was a gentleman with shoulder length hair with me, who had lost a great deal of weight before he passed over. He said this man had worn a uniform with a peak cap when he was younger. I knew exactly who he was talking about and was willing him to say his name. He talked about a photo of the spirit gentleman and me as children and as he described it, I was blown away. I didn't need to hear his name, I already carried it in my heart. The gentleman he had been describing was my eldest brother John who had recently gone to the spirit world. He had been a soldier when he was younger so that explained the uniform. John had lost a huge amount of weight whilst he was ill and a few days before he passed, I took him a photo of the two of us of when we were very young. Colin described the photo to a tee, even talking about the pattern on the wallpaper at the back of the shot. I was so happy to know John was now pain free and settled in the spirit world.

# Chapter 8
## Learning from the great and the good

Throughout the years, I have been able to improve my mediumistic abilities by learning with the great and the good. In 2010, I was lucky enough to undertake a three-day seminar with Tony Stockwell, a well-known spirit medium. This was the first of many times I would learn from Tony. Tony has written a number of books on mediumship, travelled the world sharing his gift and spent a number of years on television, doing programmes like passing over and psychic detective. Tony taught me how to polish my messages and how to strengthen my links with those in the spirit world. We were given exercises to do in groups and in pairs.

In one exercise, we were split into groups and told to do a demonstration of mediumship with each member giving a message. This time, though, we were told to bring a spirit through but not to stop there and to ask the spirit to bring those who were with them through too. My teaching mode kicked in and I got our group organised sorting which order we would get up to demonstrate. There were some really strong messages linked to people in the 'audience'. Some of the group, were able to bring through husbands and wives, aunties and uncles and even mothers and their children. When it was my sister's turn to get up, she described a lady from the spirit world. She then said there was a man with her with a wooden leg. Everyone burst out laughing but one of the group said, they knew who this was! Apparently, it was her great grandad who had lost a leg in the First World War. Her lovely one-legged relative went on to bring guidance to her about an issue she was facing. It is amazing what information you can get when you push yourself.

On the second evening of the seminar, Tony said he would do a short demonstration of physical mediumship. I had read about this phenomenon before, but I had never seen it done live. Tony closed the curtains behind him and sat on a table. There were about sixty of us, all sitting on chairs in rows, anticipating what we would see. I was kneeling on a chair at the back of the group and Eileen, my sister, was sitting to the side of me. As we watched, Tony went into a deep trance and, as he sat there, you could visibly see his features start to change. Rather than a man sitting there, you could see the features of a women building. I was particularly drawn to looking at Tony's hands; they had completely changed, becoming thinner with longer fingers and nails. His features changed a couple of times more to those of males and just before he finished, a final spirit began to materialise. Eileen nudged me and whispered, "It's dad." I couldn't believe my eyes; my dad was standing there looking over at us. The shock and disbelief of what we were seeing left me glued to my chair, I just couldn't move. I gave my phone to my sister and told her to go and get a photograph. Dad had passed over several years before and to see him so clearly again was mind blowing to say the least. Dad started to fade and within a minute or, so Tony was looking like himself again and back in the room. Eileen had managed to get a photo of dad. We had been asked not to use flashes during the demonstration and, although Eileen and I can tell it is definitely dad, the photo is a little dark and grainy. I am hoping one day to get the quality of the picture professionally enhanced.

At another of Tony's seminars, he invited another quite well-known medium, David Holt, to assist with some teaching. In the evening, Tony and David arranged to do a public demonstration of mediumship. Not only the members of the class would attend but it was open to the public too. The room was busy that evening with around two hundred and fifty people packed in. Tony rolled out the messages including bringing through one lady's daughter who sadly had been murdered.

When it was David's turn, he too gave several messages to people in the audience. He then said he had a flamboyant young man in his mid-twenties with him. He went on to describe the spirit he was working with and said he was a musician. By now my ears had pricked up and I thought that sounded like Glyn. Glyn had been passed over for about twenty-five years by then. David asked if anyone could recognise who he was talking about? I put my hand up and said yes. He went on to provide more information about Glyn's passing and said he was now working in the spirit world helping other young people adjust once they found themselves there. This was amazing. Although I had seen Glyn's hands playing the keyboard all those years ago, I had heard very little from him since. I found the whole experience so uplifting and was glad to know Glyn had found his true vocation in the afterlife.

In 2016, I was blessed to do a course with one of the world's most resound psychic mediums, James Van Praagh. He was on a tour of Britain having travelled from his home in America. I had read a lot of James's work. He is the author of several books and, for years, I had used one of his meditation texts to help strengthen my psychic and mediumistic faculties. His little book of meditations is a really good text for anyone starting out on their spiritual journey. In one of the exercises he set, we were asked to do a trance dance. I had never heard of this before. We were assured that swaying side to side whilst listening to spiritual music would help us to feel much closer to spirit. I was a bit sceptical but found a space on the floor and joined in. As I closed my eyes and began the exercise, I started to feel a great lightness around me; my arms began to rise up without effort and stretch out like a bird. I could feel someone holding my hands. As I asked in my mind who it was, I started to smell pipe smoke and I knew straight away who this was; it was my pop, he loved his pipes when he was younger. On the other side of me I could sense my nan. I have never felt this level of closeness to spirit before. I was standing on my tiptoes, arms outstretched, holding on to the hands of my departed grandparents. After this exercise, I felt like a big weight had been lifted from my shoulders and from then on, I started to feel lighter and brighter and able to feel spirit so much easier.

I will forever be grateful to these great teachers for helping me hone my mediumistic skills. I always wanted to do a course with Colin Fry too but sadly he passed away too soon after being struck down with terminal lung cancer. I never say never because, who knows, I might get the pleasure of meeting him in the next life.

It's not just learning from other mediums that helps with spiritual development, it is also the lessons learned in life. There have been many times in my life where I have had to use true grit to get through situations presented to me, like losing lots of loved ones, fighting off illness and, yes, temporary homelessness. It is only whilst I have been on my spiritual journey, that it dawned on me I have had to face all these things, so I can empathise with others who seek my help. The spirit world has a strange way of helping us to learn that whatever we go through there is always a lesson to be learned from it.

By 2016, I was getting even busier with readings and wished it was possible to do this as a full-time job.

Don't get me wrong, I still enjoyed working with the students at university, but I was now fifty-seven years old and the travelling, especially the crowded trains, was starting to get me down. I couldn't justify walking away from a career it had taken me so many years to build and I knew if it was meant to be the spirit world would help set the conditions for it to materialise. Gary and I had recently moved house and it cost more than the last one. Although we only had a small amount of mortgage left to pay, I felt I needed to continue working till it was finally paid off. I cracked on like I always had, balancing my spiritual work with my academic career.

In October of the same year, I met my mum for lunch, kissed her goodbye when we finished and headed off to my car that was parked in an underground car park. It had been a very wet day; the rain hadn't stopped for hours. To get down to the car park I needed to go down a travelator. I got about two-thirds of the way down when I slipped, my feet went from under me, and I came crashing down with a bump. I jumped up and felt a sharp pain in my buttock. I now knew what people meant when they referred to a pain in the bum. As I got up, a security guard came dashing to my aid. I felt embarrassed that, on the security camera, he had seen me fall; I just wanted to get in my car and go home. He insisted I was checked over by the first aider and put my details in the accident book. Eventually I got home.

The following morning, when I went to get out of bed the pain in my lower back was crippling and I felt like I had torn a ligament in my leg. I visited my GP and he confirmed I had knocked my spine and now had a bulging disc. He also confirmed ligament damage in my leg. The fall had caused more damage than I originally thought. I had physiotherapy for weeks and needed crutches to aid my walking for over two years. I was still going up and down to university on the train and walking back up the hill after work to the station was a killer. I could barely walk fifty metres without having to stop for a rest due to the excruciating pain in my back and leg. Eventually, with the help of painkillers, my back problem became bearable but the pain in my buttock and leg seemed to be getting worse. It wasn't just when I tried to walk that my leg hurt but also when I lay down in bed. We were going through a particularly busy time at work, and we were short staffed so going off sick wasn't an option; students were relying on me for dissertation supervision and their examination preparation. I struggled on, working from home whenever I could.

After almost two years of this, I was getting weary, and I called on the spirit world for help. I was sitting at my desk at work a few weeks later when an email caught my eye. The university was looking for people to take voluntary redundancy. I looked through the conditions and the renumeration package looked good. I had also paid extra into my pension for over twenty years, so it was affordable and worth considering. I asked for further details then filled in the application form. Before

I knew it, I was serving out my three months' notice after over twenty-five years working at the university I was going to be on my way. I am sure the spirit world had a hand in facilitating this, and at last I was free to spend more time on my mediumship and healing.

This part of my journey, however, wasn't quite over. I woke up one morning to find my leg had swollen overnight and I couldn't feel any sensation in my foot. It was back to the doctors for me. This time I saw a different GP. He did some tests and sent me for a scan. Within days I was sitting opposite a vascular surgeon. He told me I had developed a blood clot in my femoral artery, possibly brought about from the fall I had taken on the metal travelator that day all that time ago. No wonder I had been in so much pain for so long! Within days I was having a procedure to remove the clot and have a stent fitted. The surgeon couldn't believe I had been hobbling around in so much pain and no one had picked it up earlier. Although I still couldn't walk as far as I used to, the pain in my leg soon subsided. The bulge in my back has been a different matter. There is no further treatment for that and, with some healing from the spirit world, it is just something I have had to live with.

I had some new business cards printed advertising my mediumship and within no time at all my diary was full of appointments for people wanting readings. The beauty of it is I don't need to run around any more; my sitters now come to me. The moral of this tale is that spirit will put the conditions in place for where you are supposed to be, and what you are meant to be doing at any given time, on this journey we call life.

# Chapter 9
## Readings

It is now thirty-seven years since I gave that very first message in the open circle at my local spiritualist church. Since then, I have had the pleasure of working with thousands of people. The sitters who seek me out come from all walks of life; rich, poor and, everyone in between. It doesn't matter who we are, none of us can hide from the emotion of grief. The one thing we all have in common is we will have loved ones in the spirit world. There is no better reward than being able to help someone who is bereaved. To see someone come through your door broken-hearted and leave feeling a bit better because they have had a message from their loved one proving life continues after physical death is amazing and something I never tire of seeing.

I have done numerous readings over the years, too many to remember, but some will stay with me forever. One night a few years ago, I was asked if I would like to go as a guest to a charity function. The function was to raise money for a young family who had lost their mum after she was killed by a lorry whilst walking her baby in the pram. I am always happy to support a good cause and was looking forward to the evening. Julie, my old spiritual teacher, was going to give a demonstration of mediumship and another medium, Peter, who could sing, was to provide the entertainment. In addition, there were to be tarot readings, a bar and a disco. I was looking forward to a night out. It had been a while since I had had the time to go out and socialise and I even thought I might have a tarot reading myself as the money raised would be going to a good cause.

As I arrived at the venue, I ran into Julie at the door. She said she was looking out for one of the tarot readers who should have been there by now. She said if they didn't turn up there would only be Jackie available to do readings and she had a lot of people wanting them. I said not to worry. If the person who should have been doing the reading didn't turn up, I would step in. Bang went my relaxing night out. Within minutes Julie came over and said the supposed reader had just rung to say they couldn't make it. I thought there must be a reason for this and asked Julie where she wanted me to set up. I was shown into a small back room that held two desks, four chairs and Jackie the other person down to do readings. As I wasn't expecting to work, I didn't have my own cards with me, so I had to borrow a set from Jackie.

The evening got going and I had a steady stream of people wanting readings. As the night came to an end the lady sitting in front of me said she thought she was the last one. I was looking forward to finishing as my last sitter left. However, just as I was going to give

Jackie her cards back and take the money I had raised to Julie, a lady popped her head around the door asking if I had got room for just one more. I looked at her quizzically; I was sure she had already been to see me earlier in the evening. She said it wasn't for her and pushed a slim young man through the door.

Before he even sat down, I could feel the anger coming from him. He said, "I don't believe in all this."

I said, "How do you know? I haven't done the reading yet." I asked him to sit down, and I would see what I could get. As he sat there, I could feel his emotions and they were changing from anger to sadness. I shuffled the cards and spread them across the desk. I asked him to choose nine cards. I thought I would start with an overview of his past, present and future. I placed the cards in groups of three and began to turn them over one by one. The first group of cards looked fine. I could see he had had a happy upbringing and a loving relationship, nothing to worry about there.

As I began to turn the cards in the next pile, which represented the present, I could see these were being far less kind than the ones already read. I could see him standing at a crossroads feeling very angry with someone. I then saw a bad accident and before I got to the last card, I could hear a voice saying, "It's Karen." Who was Karen? This wasn't making a lot of sense, so I asked him to give me a minute whilst I tried to sort out what I was seeing and what the cards were trying to say. I then saw a young spirit lady materialising at the side of my sitter. She said she was Karen and she belonged to him. I then heard a screeching noise and a loud bang in my head. The penny dropped. This guy in front of me was the husband of the girl who had been killed by the lorry, the same one this charity evening was all about.

I hesitated for a few seconds before I spoke. Was he ready to hear this? He seemed really angry and might punch me or something if I said she was here. Karen said to tell him she was upset with what he was thinking of doing and not to do it because the children needed him even more, now she had gone. I pushed my chair back to make a bit more space between us just in case he jumped up. I had a quick think and thought she wouldn't have come through if he wasn't ready for the message. I took a deep breath and started to describe Karen who was standing at his side. I told him, "She says she belongs to you, and she asks you stop being angry and not to carry out what you have planned." She said she loved him and the children very much and would always be around them in spirit until they were reunited when it was his time to join her. She said, tell him to always wear the bracelet and then she left. As I told him she was around him and what she had said, I could see the stress and anger fade from his face now Karen had been in touch. Tears began to roll down his checks and I moved round the desk to comfort him. He was releasing all his anger and hate. He couldn't thank me enough and said he felt so much better now he knew she was all right. I asked him what he was planning to do, and he told me he was trying to track the lorry driver down and he was going to kill him. I reminded him what Karen had said and he assured me he wouldn't do it now.

I advised him to go home and do the best he could for his beautiful children. He said, "That's exactly what I'm going to do."

As I left the room and entered the main hall, I saw him telling a group of ladies what had just happened. He shouted, "Thank you, love" across the room to me and smiled. I said it was no problem, I was only the medium, it was Karen he needed to thank. He went off into the night looking so much lighter and I never saw him again. I thought it was strange I had found a spare night to come here, but, of course, spirit had guided me here to give this very important message. The spirit world never ceases to amaze me.

On another occasion, a lady contacted me in a right state. She said she hadn't been able to sleep for weeks and was sobbing. She said she had lost someone who she loved dearly but didn't elaborate. I broke my own golden rule and arranged to fit her in after the other readings I had booked in for that night. It was obvious she needed to see me and was desperate for a reading. When she arrived, I made her feel comfortable and began the reading. I could see she was dark under the eyes and looked racked with grief. I began to see balloons around her and as I looked at them, they began to change to the shape of letters. I could clearly see they were spelling out the name Paul. I asked her did she know a Paul in the spirit world? She burst out crying and said, "Yes, I do."

As I was asking this question, I could feel a restricted feeling around my neck. I just knew whoever Paul was, he had hung himself. I asked Paul to come closer to me so he could link with the lady sitting opposite me. I saw a picture of a handsome young man with light coloured hair drawing close. He was calling out, "Mum, Mum." I told my sitter I had her son with me and how he had passed over. She confirmed it was him. He said he was sorry and thanked her for the balloons, he had seen them being released after his funeral. He said, "Tell her I love her, but my head was in a bad place." He confirmed he was now with his nan in the spirit world, and all was well.

I passed this information on to the sitter and as I did, I could see a weight lift off her shoulders. I said, "You know he is safe now and he lives on forever in the spirit world." She said it had made her feel so much better knowing he was okay and now with her mother.

As she was leaving, she said, "I can't thank you enough."

I told her, "Don't thank me, thank Paul. He is the one who used so much energy to come through tonight." She then told me he had got involved with the wrong crowd and had been heavily into taking drugs. He had owed money to drug dealers all over the place and couldn't see any way out. I gave her a hug and said, "I know you will sleep better tonight." I couldn't change the ending of Paul's life journey on earth, but I had managed to reunite him with his mother again from the spirit world, even if only for a short time. She went off into the night looking a lot less strained than when she had come in and that's why I do what I do.

I was taking the service one night at the local spiritualist church when a spirit lady with blond wavy hair started to build. I was drawn to two ladies sitting at the back of the congregation. I asked them if I could work with them, and they said yes. The spirit lady was taking me to a shop in a road in the local vicinity. I asked the two ladies if this meant anything to them and they said it did. As I said this, I could see the lady from the spirit world doing piles and piles of ironing. I told them what I saw, and they both began to laugh. I thought, have I got it wrong? Was this not coming from the spirit world? Just as I was thinking this, the lady in the spirit world said, "They know who I am and tell them if they don't stop falling out, I will bang their heads together."

After the service, I was drinking a cup of coffee when the two ladies I had given the message to came over. They thanked me for the message and said the lady I had brought through was their mum. She used to run an ironing service from a shop in the road I had mentioned, and they knew what she meant about banging their heads together. Apparently, since the lady had passed on the two ladies, who turned out to be sisters, had been disagreeing about who got what share of their mother's belongings following her passing.

Another time a lady consulted me and as I began to tune in, I could see a smart-looking gentleman from the spirit world building. He was wearing a badge on his lapel in the shape of wings. I immediately knew there was a connection to the air force. I described the spirit gentlemen and told her about the badge. She confirmed it was her husband who had passed a couple of years ago. I asked him why he had come and what was the message he wanted me to pass on? He said, "tell her, I'm sorry. I didn't know what I was doing and tell her to stop beating herself up. I forgive her for putting me in the home." I passed this message to the sitter, and I could see the relief on her face. My sitter told me later that in the latter phase of his life her husband had dementia. She did her best to look after him, but he had started to get violent. One day, he pushed her away and she fell, badly breaking her arm. After that she had become frightened of him and although she had promised him, she would never put him in care, she couldn't go any further and found him a place in a residential care home. Since his passing, she had felt racked with guilt that she hadn't been able to look after him at home till the end. Another sitter who left feeling happier than when she arrived.

One of the nicest messages I have given to date was when baby M came through to me. Baby M was the little boy born with the genetic condition who I referred to earlier. His mum had come to me in a depressed state and asked if I could try and get a message for her. I explained I can't just call up particular spirits, they contact me, not the other way round. I said I would see what I could do but couldn't promise anything. I got into meditation mode and called out to baby M in my mind. I could see him clearly playing in the spirit world with two other children, who he said were his brother and sister, and a lady with the same name as his mum was looking over them. I thought this couldn't be right. He said to tell mummy he loved the teddy bear. I apologised to his mum and told her I couldn't get much but I could tell her what I got. I explained I had seen him playing with the other children he said were his brother and sister and the name of the lady looking after them. I then mentioned the teddy he said he liked, and she burst into tears. I thought she must be upset because I hadn't been able to get much for her. On the contrary, she said she had two more children in the spirit world, the lady I mentioned was her aunt and the teddy bear I referred to was the headstone in the shape of a teddy she had just ordered! I was blown away and so happy I had been able to reunite this little angel with his mum, even if only for a few minutes.

# Chapter 10
## Becoming spiritual

We are not humans having a spiritual experience but spirit having a human experience. From spirit we come and to spirit we will return. The death of the human body is inevitable. Once we have had the experiences and learned the lessons we have come here to learn, the body is shed, and the energy of the spirit goes on. How do I know this, I hear you cry? I have been taught this by my spiritual guides and teachers in the spirit world. Most people live their lives in the heavy energy of life, oblivious to the spirit world until they return there following physical death. Some, on the other hand, bring the knowledge of spirit with them after birth. How many children do you know who have an 'imaginary friend'? As children in the western world, we are socialised to believe there is no such thing as spirit and those that children may see in their early years are just pretend or make-believe. If we look at indigenous populations, such as aborigines, the opposite is true; communication with ancestors is the norm.

We are all born with a sixth sense, that of intuition, and are capable of mediumship, but in western societies this is not encouraged. People are persuaded to engage with modes of capitalism and consumerism, not with the afterlife and spirits.

Each and every one of us has the capacity to communicate with the spirit world, we just need patience and practice. Some would have you believe mediumship is a special gift only bestowed on a few; there is nothing further from the truth. Lots of people are happy to go through life and not give the afterlife a single thought until they arrive there following their passing. For others, it is an awakening usually guided by spirit. Most mediums are guided by spirit to spiritual sites of learning such as spiritual churches, centres, demonstrations of mediumship, a given book on the topic or a spiritual website. Those who are chosen to do such work will always be guided to the right place at the right time. This is not to say you can't find your own path. I would suggest, however, that you don't go it alone in early development. By all means do some spiritual meditation to open your mind to spirit but when you want to practice your craft it is always advisable to do so with someone more experienced. Contact your local spiritualist church, join an open circle or find a suitable development group.

Being a spirit medium is much more than giving messages, it is a way of life and the more you develop your own brand of spiritualism the clearer your mediumship will become. I am not suggesting you need to behave like an angel. You are, after all, a spirit having a human experience and none of us are perfect. I myself was quite a selfish person in my early years; then, everything was about me, and I worshipped materialism. I had to have the latest gadget and the best of fashion. I only learned from my spiritual awakening, following some bad experiences, that there is more to life than my wants and needs. You will find the more you give of yourself to others, the more good will come to you. Believe me, this is the law of the universe. What you give will come back tenfold. Being spiritual isn't about been a goody-goody, it is being conscious of the world around you and the people in it. It is about becoming empathetic, understanding, seeing the bigger picture and helping others around you. This doesn't need to be in a material way. It might just be a kind thought or sending out healing thoughts to the sick and the lonely. If people on earth don't want to be around you because you may be selfish or uncaring, why would spirit want to be around you either?

My journey to mediumship has been a rocky one. I had to experience many things; bereavement, trauma, illness, and homelessness to name a few, but this has taught me invaluable lessons. I thought at the time of these events, why me? These days I am grateful for the experiences I endured. They have taught me lessons that have made me the kind, empathetic and spiritual person I have become today. We all have problems throughout this life; it is, I'm afraid, part of the fabric of the human condition. It is how we react to such problems that's the key. We can become bitter and twisted or we can learn and grow from the situations we go through. I know which one I would prefer to do. You don't necessarily need to be spiritual to become a medium, but it would be like learning ballet; without precision, you can do the steps but the dance as a whole will be poor.

Good mediumship does not happen overnight, it needs to be developed alongside personal growth. Most good mediums stay in development for a lifetime. I suggest if you are drawn to this path, you start small and aim big. Early steps should start with regular meditation. This will clear out lots of unnecessary thoughts and clear space for spirit to use your faculties. I can't emphasise enough that spiritual development is not a sprint; it is more of a gentle jog. Set your intentions and be prepared to be patient; Rome wasn't built in a day. Ask yourself why you want to do this? If it is for fame and fortune, forget it, it is all about serving spirit, not your bank account. There are a few people out there who have become rich through their mediumship, but they are few and far between and none have set out with the intension of making money. It is the clarity of the messages they deliver that has made them famous. They have put the groundwork in just like any other budding medium.

Work on yourself, as well as your mediumistic development, face your own shortfalls and work on them. Let any me, me, me thoughts go and replace them with the intention of helping others. As I have already said, when you give to others the rewards will come back to you. This may not be by way of financial gain, but it will certainly bring more self-satisfaction. The more you share your positive energy with others the closer the spirit world will be able to come to you. It's all about raising your vibrations. A good place to start is by sending good thoughts out to others. Wish people well even if you don't agree with them. Remember, everyone who crosses our life comes either as a blessing or as a lesson. Send out healing thoughts to people who are ill, lost or lonely; this doesn't cost anything and can be very beneficial to the recipient. Join an online healing circle; you will be amazed how many people out there are asking for help. I know it's a big ask but try not to be bitter about the bad things that happen in your life, embrace them as lessons, grow from them and move on.

Don't let other people put you off. Not everyone will understand what you are trying to do, that's okay, it isn't their journey. People may ridicule you or think you are a bit strange. Let them think what they like and remember you shouldn't worry about what others think of you. It is only their lack of knowledge that brings them to such conclusions. Don't shout it from the rooftops every time you do a good deed, keep it between you and the recipient; the rest of the world doesn't need to know. If you are doing good deeds with the expectation of a reward, you are not doing it right. Give for the sake of giving and your needs will be met. Set the right intentions, proceed with love in your heart and watch your spiritual development grow.

Find a group to help hone your development; working with like-minded people will raise your confidence. A good place to start is the open circle at your local spiritualist church. You can practice giving messages in a safe and mutual environment. It doesn't matter if you don't give messages at first, just sitting in the circle and watching others will lift your vibrations. When you become confident enough to stand up and give a message from the spirit world, don't worry if it's not perfect, practice makes perfect, and everyone needs lots of practice before they become proficient in communicating with spirit. You may, at first, just see an object or hear a word, but, however small, give it to the sitter, you will be surprised at how many people will understand what you are saying and be able to take comfort from it. In my own early years of development one of the first messages I gave was to describe in detail a brooch that I could see in my mind's eye. I described what I had seen to the circle and a lady stood up and said she could take that. It was her departed mother's brooch I had described, and she had only been looking at it the day before! So, don't be disappointed if you don't initially get much information, it may not mean a lot to you but the person receiving the message will be delighted. With time and patience, the messages will become stronger and more informative. Practice makes perfect, so keep practicing, practicing and more practicing. Practice leads to perfection.

Once you have being doing your awareness of the spirit world in the open circle for a while, the chances are you will be invited to sit in the church development circle or even a home development class. These are usually run and overseen by a practicing medium with plenty of experience. The development circle or class will do what it says on the tin; it will help you to develop your skills and enable you to give clearer messages. Most development circles start by teaching you about the history of spiritualism, the pioneers who have led the way. You will then be taught about the different faculties, sight, hearing, smell, etcetera and how spirit use our faculties to relay the message through our senses. You will learn to improve your meditation skills and give clearer messages. This is an ongoing process that may last for many years. Again, the more you sit in the power of spirit, the more proficient you will become in your mediumship. Such groups ultimately give you space to blend with the spirit and learn how to work for them in a clear communicative manner.

Eventually, you can take your learned ability beyond the circle and start to practice your craft on friends and family. Write down the messages you deliver and go back and see if they could have been delivered more clearly. Spirit will also sometimes give you symbols to work with, so learn how to interpret them. For example, you may be shown a Christmas tree and a funeral procession. What does this mean to you? I would interpret this as a death of a loved one who belongs to the sitter passing over around the Christmas period. I would then ask the spirit world in my mind to give me more information. I may see a lady, a gentleman or young person building in my mind, and I would give this information to the sitter. I would describe the spirit person I was seeing then ask them how they are known to the sitter. I might, for example, see a vision of my own mother in my mind. I would use this as a reference point and know I had the sitter's mother with me. I would continue to ask spirit for a message. Why have they made this contact and what is it they have come to say? I would pass on the information to the recipient and the message would be concluded.

I always teach my students there are three parts to a good message. I call this the DEM method. D is for description; firstly, describe the spirit person you are seeing. E is for evidence; provide evidence to show that this is the person their loved ones need to hear from. This could be a number of things, the condition of the illness they had before they passed over, a memory link, a description of something they have left behind or a memory of a happy time they spent with the sitter. Finally, M is for message; ask the spirit person why they have come and what the message is they want to send. Provide the sitter with all the information and the message is complete. It may sound complicated but if you break it down into the three sections outlined above you should conclude with a clear and meaningful message.

Eventually, when you have had lots of practice and feel more confident, move on to doing readings for people you don't know. Spread the word that you are available for readings, advertise and distribute some cards with your information printed on them.

I wish you luck on your spiritual path. If spirits want you to work for them, they will never let you down. Stay humble and don't let your ego get the better of you. You may have learned a great skill but don't get too carried away with it. Remember, a medium is but the person delivering the message, it is the spirit world that does all the hard work. Think of yourself as a phone, a way of communicating. Remember, though, a phone can break down if not treated properly. Respect the spirit world and the people on earth you are privileged to serve, and you will go far.

# Chapter 11
## Moving forward

We are now well into the twenty-first century. The world has witnessed one of its worst events in history. We have been through one of the worst pandemics since the Spanish flu that ravished the earth over a hundred years ago. The first case of COVID-19 was witnessed in China before spreading to all corners of the globe. Millions of people have been ill or succumbed to death because of this virulent disease. Is this a case of the earth getting its own back? I think so. Overt consumerism and the overuse of harmful products like oil and plastics has consumed the world with toxins and the death of much wildlife. Thankfully, many governments across the world are now beginning to tackle this problem by compulsory reducing the use of plastics and setting goals to reduce harmful emissions by 2050. A new vaccine has been developed to protect us from the dreaded coronavirus. Those who have been locked down in their homes to protect them against the virus are once again free. Let's hope we have all learned a lesson from this, I know I certainly have. Treat the world with respect and kindness and it will respect you back. Abuse the earth and it will abuse you back. It really is that simple.

I woke up one day to find I am now in my sixties and entering the final quarter of my life on earth. Life passes by very quickly, so embrace it. Be glad for the life you have been given because, believe me, there will always be someone worse off. Don't take yourself too seriously and try to enjoy your journey. Be grateful for the people around you. They may have been sent as a blessing or to teach you a lesson. Whatever it is, embrace it, learn from it and keep moving forward.

My fall in 2016 was by no means an accident. The spirit world had new work for me to do and by 2018, having hobbled about on crutches up and down to work for two years, the penny finally dropped. The spirit knew there was no way I would give up the career I loved without putting in place the conditions to force me to rethink. It wasn't a coincidence when I was offered voluntary redundancy by the university, spirit had a hand in this too.

After my retirement, I immediately had so much more time on my hands, something I had never known as I had worked in one guise or another since I was fifteen years old. I instinctively knew what I had to do, I got some business cards printed, set up the readings by Rita website, a Facebook page and away I went. My main job was now working as a spirit medium. People have never stopped contacting me since. I am now doing the job I was always destined to do. My past job as a lecturer had stood me in good stead, I was already used to working with people from all walks of life. These days I go through life at a slower pace, I have had to learn to put the brakes on if I want to keep well. I now do my spirt work part-time and spend the rest of the time on hobbies and enjoying life with Gary, who has now retired too. I have at last found my work/life balance.

Due to the pandemic and being unable to mix with others under government's restrictions, I have been unable to do one-to-one readings in person, but this hasn't stopped the demand for my services. I have embraced technology and moved the readings online. I was initially surprised by the demand and the quality of the readings; I was worried the quality of the readings would abate. I really had no need to worry. If the spirit world has a message to give, they will deliver it by any means. I now enjoy doing online readings, I can relay the connection between loved ones in the spirit world and the recipient without compromising the health and safety of the sitter or my family.

The home development circle sadly had to be put on hold for a couple of years due to government legislation that stopped people meeting up in each other's houses. However, nothing is lost; spirits are always working on our development in the background anyway. Thankfully. Since March 2022 there are no more restrictions on how many people can meet up together and the development group can once again meet in person. The group have had some amazing evidence of life after death throughout the years we have sat together in the circle.

Given my past health record, I am very much into self-care these days. To feel healthy in mind and body aides the delivery and clarity of spirit messages. For the first twelve months or so since I left the university, I fell into the trap of overeating. With all the extra time on my hands, it was easy to enjoy all the extra food I now had time to eat. I would think nothing of having breakfast, afternoon tea with lots of cake, dinner and then snacks in the evening. Before I knew it, I had put on over two stones. The strain on my back from carrying the extra weight led to me hobbling about again and been unable to walk very far before I was in severe pain. I spoke to my spirit guides and asked for help. Over six months I lost two and a half stones and took up swimming. Swimming is a non-weight bearing exercise so suits my condition well. I regularly swim now and feel so much better for it. A healthy mind and body lead to clearer communication, something that is very useful in my line of work.

Gary and I have always loved gardening but in the past never had as much time to do it as we would have liked. These days, weather permitting, we are always out pottering in the garden. We now grow tomatoes and vegetables. There is a sense of joy watching something grow from seed into a beautiful flower or fruit. I have always enjoyed being out in nature ever since I was little, and my brother John and I played on the hills with our pretend 'magic carpets'. To sit in nature and feel the sun on your face is a great natural healing pastime, which I would recommend to anyone feeling under the weather. I have a meditation bench in my garden, and I have received some of the best spirit communications ever when sitting there.

I have been blessed in life to have two lovely grandsons. They have enriched my world and we have done so many wonderful things together. We have had lots of holidays and days out over the years, and I owe it to them for keeping me young at heart. They are both now growing into fine young men. Both are at college and finding their place in the world. The years I have had with them have brightened my life. Time has flown by; it only seems like yesterday I was changing their nappies. I need to thank my daughter Nicola for bringing these two bundles of light into the world. Their other grandma now resides in the spirit world, but I know she has watched them grow and will always looks over them.

I have met some wonderful people on this journey we call life and I have been blessed to enjoy the enrichment they have brought me. It is through our interactions with others that we learn and grow, and I have learned so much from those I have encountered. I must admit there have been some people on my path I could have quite happily have strangled, but I now know such people were brought to teach me too. The knowledge of human life has put me in good stead when teaching or doing my spirit work. Not everyone in life will be kind to you. Sadly, this too is a much-needed lesson, even if they have only taught us how not to behave, they too have done their job. There are just too many people who have enriched my life to mention here, but you all know who you are, and I thank you. It is almost Christmas as I write this chapter; always a good time to reflect on what has gone and what is yet to come. I always spend time thinking about my friends and loved ones who have gone to the spirit world before me. I don't feel sad, I know they have been here to earth to learn lessons. Once those lessons were learned they return back to the spirit world. I know we all make a contract with our spirit guides before we come to the earth plane. We decide what we want to learn and how we are going to do it before we return to the spirit world. All this learning helps spirit progress in the spirit world. For example, I now know why my brother Glyn died suddenly so young; he wanted to go through this experience himself to get a good overview of what it is like to live a short life. This has helped him lots. His work now is to help young people who go over to adjust to their new life in the spirit realms.

As always, I continue to learn and grow. Recently I have completed a twelve-month mentorship programme with one of the world's leading mediums, the wonderful Gordon Smith. For homework, he asked that we ask the spirit world a question and wait for the answer. I asked spirit what I should do next. The answer came back quickly. I was told to write a book, hence why you are reading these pages now. With guidance and inspiration, the words have come easily, showing once again what can happen when you put your trust in spirit. I have read many of Gordons books and they have helped me, and my development students go from strength to strength. I have been blessed to have been taught by the best, Gordon, Tony, James and David among others. They have all contributed to the style of mediumship I practice today, and I wish to thank them all.

Alongside readings, I am also in great demand for spiritual healing. I do lots of aura cleansing and repairs. If the aura, that's the energy field around us, is damaged, the body and the mind will be too. I have seen some fabulous results when using the methods bestowed upon me by spirit. Just like my mediumship, I am only the go-between for the two worlds; the real work done through me is credited to the spirit world.

I have had a varied and interesting journey in this life so far and I hope to stay here a while longer in the service of spirit but when I am called home, I will feel no fear. I already know my spirit will live on and I will be reunited with my loved ones who have gone over before me. Whilst I am still here, I like to keep in touch with all the people I love. During lockdown, when we were instructed to stay at home due to the coronavirus, I managed to keep abreast of what my loved ones were doing through social media. I know there is a downside to some of these sites, but they have their uses too. You will often find me in the evening with my laptop switched on following folk online. I watch how my youngest brother Robert is doing with his fishing; he's an avid fisherman. I might message my other brother David and his beautiful wife, Heather for a chat and last, but not least, I like to follow my gorgeous sister Eileen's page. She is my angel here on earth and has been my rock since the day she arrived in this world.

Twenty-seven years since I put it to one side, I have finally looked at my PhD again. Who knows, if I find the time, I might even finish it. Life is for living, so make sure you cram everything in, life on earth is short but the spirit goes on to eternity.

I hope you have enjoyed reading my story. If I had my time again, I wouldn't change a thing. This roller coaster which we call life has been invaluable and, if I had to, I would do it all again. I am now a fully-fledged medium, an ambassador for spirit. May this journey continue from here into eternity. I thank you for showing an interest in my story and, for anyone who has been inspired to investigate spiritualism and mediumship further, there are a few exercises in the next chapter I hope will help you on your way.

# Chapter 12
## Exercises

**Meditation**

This practice can be done with or without background music. If you go for music, choose spiritual meditation music. You can find lots of good examples of this on YouTube and other sites.

Sit comfortably in a chair, keep your back and head as still as you can. Sit with your hands on your lap facing upwards and your feet flat on the floor. Close your eyes. Take a deep breath so you can feel your chest expanding then release the air by breathing out. Repeat this breathing method three or four times. Breathe normally and shift your attention to the rise and fall of your breath. Visualise a bright white light surrounding your body. Become grounded by placing imaginary threads from your spine going deep down into the earth and attaching to a boulder. Feel the energy of mother earth coming up the threads and filling your body. Feel a green healing light coming through the crown of your head. Let this light blend with the energy of mother earth that is now running through you. Quieten your mind. Let any thoughts you have just pass through the mind and don't try to analyse them. Next, silently ask your spirit guide to come close to you. Feel for any change in sensations around the body and face. You may start to feel warm or cold, you may feel tingling in a certain point of the body, or it may feel like someone is stroking your hair. Feel the sensation and note it. When you repeat this exercise again see if you get the same sensation. If you do, it means you have made your first link with your spirit guide. Sit quietly for five minutes just getting used to the change of energy around you and see any symbols or words being given to you. Breathe deeply into the lungs again three times and release any tension you may still be holding in the body. Slowly open your eyes and make notes of any sensations, symbols or messages received. Such notes will help with your progress and be a record of how far you have come on your journey since you began.

Once you are confident with your meditation and have been regularly practicing it, begin to ask questions about your spirit guide, ask for a name and any other information they might like to bestow on you. Begin to treat your spirit guide like he or she is your new best friend. You may not have had any contact with them before starting this practice, but they have known you and your spirit since before you were born. They have been assisting you and guiding you throughout your journey here on earth and will be only too glad to converse with you. Your spirit guide will work as your gatekeeper to the spirit world and help you bring messages from spirits to your sitters.

It is a good idea to ask your spirit guide to give you some confirmation that they are really around you and it is not just your imagination. Pick a symbol, such as a star, feather, a heart; more or less any symbol that comes to mind. Ask your guide to make these symbols materialise in your everyday life. If you recall, I saw a star on the floor when I left a train to go for a very important interview. I just knew my guide had placed it there for me to see as reassurance she was around me. I knew one hundred percent it was Savanna, because we had agreed in meditation, this would be her confirmation sign to show me she was near me. I had seen stars, paper ones, metal ones, stars in pictures or even star-shaped leaves, many of these in very unexpected places. Give it a try, you will be amazed by the confirmation you receive. Once you have got this far, it is a good idea to try out other meditations until you find one that resonates with you. I would recommend trying guided meditations by Tony Stockwell, Gordon Smith or James Van Praagh; all can be found on the internet.

**Working on self**

In addition to doing your meditation on a regular basis, it is important to work on yourself. Make a list of all your traits. Is there something about yourself you are not happy with? Perhaps you are short tempered, impatient or not good at sharing? Whatever parts of your personality are negative, learn to face them and work on improving them. Send out healing thoughts to others who are in need. Not only will this help them, it will benefit you too. Do small acts of kindness for others without expecting anything in return. This will help to lighten your soul; the lighter the soul, the easier the communication with spirit will be.

**Improving the message**

Once you have got used to meditating, feeling your guide around you and working on those negative traits, you will be ready to practice giving spirit messages. Remember this is not a race. Developing good mediumship is a lifetime's work. You are not going to get perfect messages every time but, with lots of practice, they will get stronger and more coherent. I would suggest if you have already come this far, now might be a good time to join a development class or circle. Alongside this, start to practice your new found craft on family members and friends. Relax, ask your spirit guide to come close, feel their 'calling card' — that's the feeling they put on you, so you know they are with you — just like you do in meditation. Once your guide is near, ask them in your mind if there is anyone in the spirit world who would like to send a message to your sitter? Wait for a response, say anything you might see, hear or feel. Is there a picture of a person in your mind's eye? Can you hear someone or smell a scent? Don't try to analyse what is being given to you, just pass the information on to the sitter. Ask the sitter if they can take any of the information being given? Do any items you may have seen hold any significance for them? This may be a bit hit and miss at first. The sitter may understand some of what you are saying but not all of it. Don't let this dissuade you. Mediumship is like a muscle; the more you practice, the stronger it becomes. Try this exercise out on as many people as you can. Tell your sitter you are just practicing; that way you will not be putting yourself under pressure to 'perform' and get everything right.

**Interpreting symbols**

On many occasions the spirit will present you with symbols, shapes, or objects. It is important that you learn how to interpret such signs. For example, if you see a daffodil, what does this mean to you? For me, it is a representation of spring. I would interpretate this to mean spring time was significant for the spirit trying to communicate. I may then be shown a coffin. I associate this with death therefore, I would link the daffodil with the coffin and say spring time was significant to the lady in the spirit world; I feel she passed in the spring. A picture of your mother may come into your mind. This is a reference point, and adds to the message, the lady who passed over in spring is your mother. You may see numbers, for example, sixty-six would suggest the spirit lady was sixty-six years old when she passed. As you can see from interpreting the signs and symbols, you can build a reliable description of the sitter's departing loved one. Different signs and symbols will be interpreted differently by different mediums. Learn what they represent for you and how to bring them together to give a coherent message. Practice makes perfect and take your time. With this tool at your disposal, you will eventually have your own library of symbols with meaningful interpretations.

**Strengthening readings**

There is a debate amongst mediums as to whether mediums should just use clairvoyance, clairaudience or clairsentience to pass on spirit messages or whether it is acceptable to blend this with other methods of divination. If you are doing a service at a spiritualist church or doing a public demonstration, it will be expected that you stick to using the clairs. When doing private readings, however, it is up to the individual medium how they proceed. All mediums are psychic but not all psychics are mediums. In my view, if you can use mixed methods to strengthen the quality of a reading you should do so. People who come for readings I find are happy to hear from their departed loved ones but also have burning issues about what is going on around them. Personally, I always start with reading the cards whilst waiting for spirit to tune in. I feel by doing so my sitters get a more rounded reading.

If you feel drawn to using tarot or even ordinary playing cards, you can learn the meanings of them from books. However, as I always tell my students, this is only someone else's interpretation. If you look at the cards in front of you and feel what they are saying you will get a much more accurate account of what is going on in the present and future of the sitter. Try doing a simple nine card reading for a friend. Shuffle the cards, pass them to the sitter and ask them to also shuffle them. Take the pack from the sitter and spread the cards face down in a line on the table. Ask your sitter to pick nine cards from the spread and keep them one on top of the other. Take the nine cards from the sitter and turn the first three cards faceup on the table. These first three cards represent the past. Look at the cards and feel what they are saying to you. Are they depicting happiness or sadness? Are you seeing people? As with the method of mediumship, say what you feel. Do the same with the second three cards. These represent the present. What do you feel is going on in the sitter's life right now? The final three cards represent the future and what is coming for the sitter. Always be sensitive about how you give the message. For example, if you see the death card in the future spread, don't assume someone is going to die, it could mean a change is coming. Always be mindful of how you phrase things.

## Asking for guidance

Spirits are not with us to solve all our problems. We are here to learn for ourselves, enjoy the good times and learn and grow from the bad. However, this is not to say we can't ask for guidance when faced with the bigger challenges of life. Go into your quiet time and meditate, ask your guide to help you find the clarity to work through the given issue. They probably won't give you an answer straight away but will help you to see the bigger picture from different perspectives; this will help you come to a clearer conclusion. Give it a try and watch your situation improve.

## Psychometry

By holding an object that belonged to a spirit, it is possible to pick up on the residual energy of the person who left the object behind after passing over. This works well with items such as jewellery that had been worn for a long time, for example, a ring or necklace. Ask your sitter to bring an item that belonged to their departed loved one to the sitting. Place the object in your hand and close your palm. Use your intuition to feel any information you are picking up. Does, the residual energy of the object imprint images of past life events on you? Say what you see and pass on this information to the sitter. Ask your sitter if they can understand the information being received. You may be surprised just how much information you can get using this method.

**Scrying**

By looking into the flames in an open fire or the flame of a candle, it is also possible to receive messages. Not many people have an open solid fuel fire these days, but a candle will do. Light a candle and stare into the flame, keeping your eyes fixed on it until you start to feel slightly mesmerised. You may see a face, a symbol or even a name. Spend five to ten minutes on this exercise. Did you receive a message for yourself or is it for one of your sitters?

**Self-healing**

Whilst you are on this journey make sure you don't forget to be kind to yourself too. It is easy to get carried away with helping others. Being a helpful psychic medium is all well and good but if you give, give, give without making time for yourself, you will eventually burn out. So, do yourself a favour and take some time for yourself. It is also a good idea to check your own aura regularly and do any necessary maintenance. This with stop you feeling drained. Sit in a chair and run your hand about three inches away from the body all round you. You will, with practice, get to know your own aura well. What do you feel as you slowly run your hand around the body? Does it feel light in parts and heavy in others? Concentrate on where you feel any heaviness. These dull sites can be the cause of aches and pain you may be having or could be the cause of emotional imbalance. It is very important you bring harmony back to optimal function because the spirit world blends with the aura when communicating with you. If it is dull, heavy or torn it will make it more difficult for spirit to work with you. Ask your guide to send you some healing. Visualise a bright green light coming through the crown of your head, fill your whole body with this light and feel it permeating out of the body into the aura. Concentrate in particular on any areas of dullness or heaviness. Shine this healing light right through such areas and feel yourself becoming lighter and brighter. Do this exercise often to maintain the status quo between the ethereal spirit of the aura and that of the physical body.

**Closing down and psychic protection**

There is a debate as to whether it is necessary to close down after working with spirit. I would argue yes, it is. You don't need protecting from the spirit world, but you do need to protect yourself and put boundaries around your mediumship. When you work with spirit, you are operating at a highly sensitive frequency. Just as you can pick up the feelings of spirit, you can pick up the feelings and emotions of other people too. As you go about your daily life, soaking up the feelings of others can be physically and mentally draining. In order to stay well and undrained, treat your mediumship like a radio; turn it on when you are working and switch it off when you finish. Different models work for different people, but I always teach the radio method to my students. When you are ready to work for spirit, send out a thought to them saying you are now available and happy to work for them. Once you have finished working, thank the spirit world for their communication and tell them you are now closing down. In your mind, visualise yourself switching a radio off. The spirit world will know you now need time to rest and recharge before undertaking the next reading or demonstration.

I hope you have found the words written here useful and I wish you well on this part of your journey we call life.

# Suggested further reading

Howarth Tomlinson, T., *Walking into the light. A seeker's guide to spiritual development* (2018). North Yorkshire, United Kingdom. 2QT Publications.

Smith, G., *Intuitive studies. A complete course in mediumship* (2012), London, England: Hay House.

Smith, G., *Spirit Messenger* (2003). London, England: Hay House.

Stockwell, T., *Spirited: Living between two worlds — a top psychic medium's extraordinary story* (2004). London, England: Hodder Publications.

Van Praagh, J., *Meditations with James Van Praagh* (2003). London, England: Random House.

# Contact the author

Website: https://www.readingsbyrita.co.uk/

https://www.facebook.com/ReadingsbyRitax/

https://www.facebook.com/Ritahaworthmedium/